The Value Network

The Value Network

Integrating the Five Critical Processes That Create Customer Satisfaction

Louis J. De Rose

American Management Association

New York • Atlanta • Boston • Chicago • Kansas City • San Francisco • Washington, D.C.
Brussels • Mexico City • Tokyo • Toronto

Library of Congress Cataloging-in-Publication Data

De Rose, Louis.
    The value network : integrating the five critical processes that
create customer satisfaction / Louis J. De Rose.
        p.   cm.
    Includes bibliographical references and index.
    ISBN 0-8144-5109-8
    1. Industrial management.   2. Consumer satisfaction.   3. Value.
I. Title.
HD31.D37   1994
658.8'12-dc20   93-43263
                                                                          CIP

Printing number

10   9   8   7   6   5   4   3   2   1

To my saintedly patient wife,
Joan,
for all the late and overcooked dinners
my writing this book has caused

Contents

The
Value
Network

Introduction

For over thirty-five years I have consulted with scores of companies in a wide range of industry. The clients I've served are in computers, electronics, electrical equipment, aerospace, heavy machinery, medical supplies, paper, chemicals, and oil refining. Within these industries I've seen practices employed in one that were little known and seldom employed in another. I've seen companies initiate policies they considered unique and enlightened, which for years had been implemented elsewhere. More and more I've come to the conclusion that very little in management theory and technique is really new.

Over these years I've also seen managements adjust to product scarcity, hyperinflation, stagflation, and periodic bouts of localized and national recession. I've seen them adapt, with varying degrees of success, to market, competitive, and technological change.

However, in recent years the extent and tempo of change has accelerated dramatically. It is evident in ever shortening product life cycles, expanding global competition, fragmenting markets, and exploding technology. It's evident in the pervasive pattern of corporate realignments, mergers and acquisitions, company downsizings and restructuring. With each successive wave of change, management's ability to adjust and adapt appears to be steadily declining.

In all my years of consulting and training experience, I have never seen management so lacking in confidence and self-assurance. I have never seen such reluctance to make critical, strategic decisions. At the same time I have never seen management so impressed by—even gullible about—theories and concepts whose main appeal is that they purport to be "new" or "advanced."

From my perspective I see an eroding of management's sense of purpose and objective. I see a loss of unifying thought about the goal of managing and the work of managing. I see a desperate search for answers—preferably, quick and easy ones—for dealing with today's business problems.

Our fascination with Japanese manufacturing methods clearly illustrates this point. Instead of contemplating the real lessons those methods convey, we dwell on apparent ones. Instead of focusing on the difficult and disciplined aspects of Japanese techniques, we embrace the simple, if not simplistic, ones.

For example, we readily accept the notion that Japanese success is attributable to "participative management"—quality circles, worker teams. This has stimulated and reinforced the notion that management is strictly a personal and interpersonal process. This has been at the expense of viewing management in terms of goals, functions, and processes. The result is poor guidance and direction of effort, aggravated by objectives that are vague and impossible to implement: "walking around management," "management for excellence," "management for excellence with a passion."

The success of Japanese manufacturing is less attributable to management's concern with human relations than it is to other factors:

- A culture and work ethic that promotes education, seeks consensus, and accepts discipline once consensus is reached
- A driving motivation to be world leaders in targeted markets and technology
- A management development process that begins with hands-on factory experience, proceeds through cross-functional training, and rewards team results rather than individual performance

These are only three factors that immediately come to mind.

We cannot change our culture, and it's doubtful we can substantially change our work ethic. But we *can* improve the effectiveness of management.

In a competitive market economy, the objective of management is to plan, organize, integrate, and measure the application of human, capital, and information resources for results. Those results are value results. *Value* means satisfying customer requirements reliably and consistently. It means satisfying them cost-effectively.

There's nothing new in this concept, in the sense that it reflects thoughts and ideas never expressed before. But it is a different concept in the sense that it takes old ideas and gives them a new focus. It sees value in terms of cost-effectiveness as the customer acknowledges or perceives it. Very few managements think about value as least total cost to the customer. Most view cost-effectiveness as the lowest cost of production and distribution. Management's orientation is for internal results, not external ones.

Further, few know how to manage for value results in the face of rapid economic and technological change. They're still wedded to outdated functional and product structures. They're still employing practices designed for another era. They don't fully understand that value can only be achieved through tightly knit networks that integrate customers and suppliers with internal value-creating and value-adding processes. My purpose in writing this book is to develop, and strongly advocate, management as the managing of that value network.

Managing for value results is a rationale that is continuing and constant. It is a rationale that provides purpose and objective, regardless of changes in the technical, economic, and competitive environment. I am convinced it's a rationale whose time has come.

Chapter 1

The Meaning of Value: Managing for Value Results

Management theory and practice do not spring from a vacuum. They emerge from wider bodies of theory and practice. These are legal, financial, and technological. They're cultural, ethical, and behavioral. They reflect society's political and economic development, society's sense of goals and values.

For good or for bad, ours is a society in constant flux. We strive for something different, something better; and we want it now. We're not a patient or conserving people. We seek instant gratification and quickly discard what we had for something new. And deluged as we are by the continuous flow of news and information, our goals and values are confused and fleeting. This is American society today. And increasingly, it's reflected in our management scene as well.

Almost daily, some "new" management theory is publicized in business journals, academic treatises, and even in the popular press. The more publicity it receives, the more it must be put into practice. Whether it is new or merely an old theory dressed up in a new acronym, is beside the point. If it appears in *Fortune* or the *Harvard Business Review*, it commands attention. And if it is the practice at companies acclaimed for excellence, then it must be copied. Unfortunately, much theory and practice proves short-lived. It's soon replaced by what is claimed to be newer, better, or quicker to achieve results.

The number of management theories and techniques American industry has developed is mind-boggling. They were introduced, practiced for a time, and then forgotten or ignored: value analysis/value engineering; managing by objectives; matrix management; strategic planning; the marketing concept. Even total quality management, which is now in vogue, has gone through several life spans. We introduced it in the 1940s, gave it further expression in the zero defect programs of the 1950s, and then forgot it. A dozen years later we reintroduced it, adapting it from Japanese manufacturers who had refined quality improvement to a fine art.

Now we see growing skepticism as to whether Japanese quality techniques really work. Quality circles, once the rage among advocates of total quality management, are being abandoned or drastically revamped in many companies.

In a *Wall Street Journal* interview, Kevin Cooney, a division vice president at Whirlpool, admitted how a decade ago he was fascinated by the notion that Japanese quality was driven by worker suggestions. Through experience, he has learned differently. He has concluded that quality circles tend to be poorly focused. They get sidetracked on minor, even irrelevant issues, like the color of paint in the washroom.[1]

Whether it's quality circles, just-in-time scheduling, or factory automation techniques, over the past two decades we have adopted, modified, even copied dozens of Japanese manufacturing methods. Without question they have produced dramatic improvements, and we've only begun to realize their full potential.

But to a restless management, it's time for change. We seek new theories, new techniques. If quality circles are old hat, try "gain sharing" or "employee empowerment." Convert the company into a "learning organization," or maybe a "virtual corporation." "Reengineer." Meanwhile, if the cold, hard facts of declining profits or increased competition intrude on the luxury of theorizing, there's always "downsizing" or plain and simple "cost cutting" to rationalize what we do.

The point of all this is that we have become profligate and petulant. We have discarded management principles and practices that are as sound today as they were when we first employed them. We have introduced change merely for the sake of change. We have become management faddists. We've been—and are being—seduced by the promise of quick-and-easy answers.

Management and "Feel-Goodism"

That search for quick-and-easy answers finds expression in the growing influence of the behavioral sciences over management theory and practice. "Management development" programs are increasingly heavy on "consciousness raising," "sensitivity training," and understanding your "psychodynamics." They stress that management's task is managing people and that how people feel is as important, if not more so, than how they think.

So good management becomes management that promotes "feeling good." Attend many of today's management seminars, and judge for yourself the subject matter and content. Listen to the questions of the human resources "facilitator": Did you enjoy the program? Did you have fun? Whether you learned anything useful to managing a business is often a secondary concern.

Personal and interpersonal skills are now the stuff of management theory. Whether the business or functional area be sales, manufacturing, or physical distribution, the route to effective management is purportedly improved skill in communication, personal motivation, and team building.

To behavioralists team building is designed to promote "corporate bonding," help develop a "corporate culture," resolve personal and group conflicts. It is directed to exploring personal attitudes and emotions as reflected in group relationships. Whether this is relevant to a company's daily business is questionable. And when it is pursued to the exclusion or subordination of real business issues, it's even more questionable. We build teams to achieve better business results, not to create a more sociable work environment.

Behavioral theory is particularly appealing. Intuitively, we all believe we have, or can acquire, skill in communicating and motivating. There's no doctoral curriculum we need to master, no apprenticeship program we successfully must complete. If managing is getting others to do what we want done—and having them "feel good" about it—that's a subject we all think we know something about.

Behavioral theory almost writes off the notion of management, as we've come to know and practice it. In its stead, business needs "leadership." Leadership connotes self-assurance, exuberance, charisma. These are all traits within our grasp, which means we all have the potential to be leaders. With a notion like this, behavioral theory is almost irresistible.

By stressing the personal, the psychological, the interrelational facets of leadership, behavioral theory gives short shrift to concerns that have always been prime concerns of management theory. Management—or leadership—of what? Toward what goals? Toward what objectives? If "leaders" don't know where they're going, or if they know but don't know how to get there, the result is chaos. Although there are some that supposedly thrive on chaos, for most companies management by chaos is not a viable option.

Getting the Wrong Answer Faster

The search for quick and easy answers finds further expression in the increasing use of computer techniques to deal with business and management issues. Where the tasks of managing— planning, scheduling, evaluating, and deciding—were once done by managers, they're now done by the computer. There is no question that this has been an incredibly positive development. The computer has vastly simplified and improved the process of managing. But in too many cases, computerizing is pursued as a quick solution to what are complex or poorly understood problems. And the results are damaging and costly.

At one heavy equipment manufacturing company I saw a materials requirements planning (MRP) system installed to deal with recurring scheduling problems. It was modelled on an IBM system designed for a warehousing and distribution business where product is bought, put on a shelf, and sold from stock. In this company there were six levels of inventory buildup, from raw material to fabricated parts to subassembly and final assembly. Needless to say, the system was a total failure. Low-cost, common-use items were constantly out of stock while inventories of high-cost, limited-use items were grossly excessive.

In a large decentralized manufacturing company, corporate MIS—with senior management approval—bought a commercially available purchasing data system. It was supposed to provide a common database for accumulating and monitoring purchase expenditures by commodity, by supplier, and by requisitioning activity. After eighteen months and nearly a quarter million dollars of out-of-pocket costs, the project had to be scrapped.

To begin with, the company had no common part numbering system. Commodities were identified differently at each using location, with no compatibility or cross-referencing mechanism in place to assimilate and track them. Second, the nature and mix of purchase transactions were too diverse from division to division for the system to be meaningful. The company had both military and commercial business, and its purchases were both for specific contract and for inventory.

These are not isolated examples of computerization gone wrong. It has been estimated that throughout the 1980s, U.S. businesses invested a staggering $1 trillion in information technology.[2] Despite the huge amounts spent, the results were disappointing. SRI International, a computer technology research firm in Menlo Park, California, publishes a quarterly journal. Its editor, Dr. Peter Neuman, identifies page after page of problems caused by computers. *The Economist,* which described Dr. Neuman's findings, called them "just the tip of the iceberg."[3]

The problem with computerization is twofold. First is the fact that those who design and program computer systems are not always knowledgeable about the business or functional areas being computerized. They too often lack the experience and insights to understand the complexities and subtleties involved. They don't always see the interrelationships between one process and another, one function and another.

The second cause of the problem lies in the fact that computer systems are designed almost as stand-alones. They're designed to plan and schedule production, monitor and control inventories, handle payrolls or accounts receivable. But there is no common management direction, no common business strategy that guides and channels the design of all systems. Thus, there is little cohesiveness in them. Even when they are integrated in networks and total business systems, they're integrated with this deficiency.

Analyzing a business problem is one thing; designing and programming a computer system to solve it is something else. Whether it's by flow chart or mathematical modelling, we can lay out in some sequential and continuous fashion a step-by-step analytical solution to the problem. Even some small error or omission does not totally invalidate the conclusions we draw.

But the discipline behind computer programming is logic, and there is no forgiving in logic. An error—even a tiny error—in one line of programming can completely throw off the entire program. When we consider that some programs can run to millions of lines, there is a distinct probability of failure. Add in system designers and programmers with little or no business or functional expertise and that probability goes up further. Factor in the lack of cohesive strategy—a logical premise—to integrate systems and programs and the probability of failure is higher still.

We have almost taken for granted the fact that computer software is prone to failure. We accept at face value that programs require "debugging"; that they require "revisions"; that they will be replaced or altered by "enhancements." What we do not question—or refuse to question—is why.

Both the behavioral sciences and computer-oriented approaches to management are deceptively appealing. They promise easy answers to the tasks of management. But unfortunately there are no easy answers. Management is not an avocation. It is the continuous and continuing process of planning, organizing, and directing human, capital, and information resources to achieve specifically defined objectives.

Management is both a science and an art. As a science it

embodies the systematic application of principles and methods that are tried and proved in practice. As an art it demands knowledge, skill, and the ingenuity to employ them creatively.

As both a science and an art, management achieves results through people. Hence, understanding human behavior and skill in human relationships are essential to management's success. Management also employs information. And it's only through advanced computer technology that management is able to collect, analyze, and disseminate the scope and volume of information vital to success in today's business environment.

But the business of management is managing business. And business is processes and functions, markets and competition. It is engineering, manufacturing, distribution and sales in different marketing arenas, under different economic conditions. It is in these areas that the behavioral sciences and computer-oriented approaches to management fall short.

Yes, There's Really a Meaning to "Value"

In his seminal work *Managing for Results*, Peter Drucker said,

> Results depend not on anybody within the business nor on anything within the control of the business. They depend on somebody outside—the customer in a market economy, the political authorities in a controlled economy. It is always somebody outside who decides whether the efforts of the business become economic results or whether they become so much waste and scrap. . . . The only thing one can say with certainty about any business activity, whether engineering or selling, manufacturing or accounting, is that it consumes efforts and thereby incurs costs. Whether it contributes to results remains to be seen.[4]

Drucker's observations, made almost thirty years ago, are as valid today as they were then. And they address the one essential too often overlooked by management faddists or those seeking quick-and-easy answers. The objective of management is results. Results are ends and outcomes. They are the consequences of actions and processes that are planned, directed, and controlled. In a free market environment, results are economic results. They are the supply of goods and services that satisfy customer requirements and are cost-effective. In a word, results supply value.

Value is one of the most frequently used words in the business vocabulary. Unfortunately, it is also one of the most vaguely defined. *Value* is used when a more appropriate term would be *price*. It's used when what we really mean is cost. It's used to mean traits as ephemeral as "high quality" or transactions as subjective as a "good deal." These are neither specific enough— nor objective enough—to identify results for which we manage. There is a definition, however, that serves that purpose. It's a definition that has evolved over the past forty-five years.

> Value is the satisfaction of customer requirements at the lowest total cost of acquisition, ownership, and use.

Value is not price. Price is only one element of cost. Total cost includes the costs of acquiring, using, maintaining, and replacing what the customer buys. It includes the costs of quality and performance failure. It includes the costs of not having quantity, time, and service requirements satisfied.

The origins of this value definition go back to 1947 with a cost improvement technique known as *value analysis*. Value analysis is an organized approach to the study of products, materials, or services in terms of needed or intended function. Its aim is to achieve that function at lowest cost. It is generally acknowledged that the formal application of value analysis started at the General Electric Company. It was initially employed on purchased materials and supplies and later extended to internally manufactured items.

In terms of reducing cost, value analysis was successful, but its limitations quickly became apparent. The problem was that value analysis was performed after components and materials had been designed and specified. This was too late in the procurement-manufacturing cycle to achieve real cost improvement. For cost improvement to be significant, value analysis would have to be done earlier in the design-engineering, manufacturing-engineering stages. Thus, value analysis developed into value engineering.

Value engineering employed the same principles as value analysis. It asked:

- What is the function that the product, component, or material must perform? Prevent corrosion? Provide insulation? Support weight?
- What design, specification, or process options are there to achieve that function?
- What does each cost?
- Which of those options achieves the desired function at the lowest cost?

It was clear that performing value analysis at the design and engineering stages was more effective than performing it later. So the discipline became more generally known as value engineering.

By about the mid 1950s, however, a problem began to surface with both value analysis and value engineering. Both techniques were employed on discrete purchased and manufactured items. These were analyzed outside the structure and context of the larger systems they comprised.

Thus, a value analysis project might achieve a "cost reduction" through source substitution. By buying to specification an equivalent pump for a dishwasher from a supplier other than the originally qualified supplier, purchasing could achieve a price reduction. Similarly, a value engineering project might achieve a "cost reduction" by designing a timer for the dishwasher that was simpler to assemble or easier to maintain.

Unfortunately, when the pump and timer were assembled or combined with other components, the dishwasher frequently failed. By changing sources or redesigning a functional component, the design integrity originally built into the machine was compromised.

It was at this point that the concept of *value systems* came into being. Value systems recognized that true cost improvement could not be achieved on a discrete part number by part number basis. Cost improvement was meaningful only on a total product, project, or system basis. Further, true cost improvement could not be achieved by any one function, or at any one stage of the business process. It could be achieved only through an organized approach that employed value analysis principles at all stages of that process, and employed them under clear management direction.

It took the development of the *marketing concept* in the early 1960s to provide the theoretical adhesive for firming up our value definition. The marketing concept says that value is acknowledged or perceived in the marketplace. It is customers who place a worth on what we supply. And they place that worth on the basis of how we meet their needs and the cost they incur in our doing so. Therefore, we must gear our business to be responsive to customer requirements. We must become market oriented, customer oriented.

With this market orientation, the notion of value is now redirected from the supplier's cost to the customer's cost. Value is not the lowest cost we incur to produce a product or service we supply. It's not the cost of the process we employ to make or distribute what we sell. Neither is value price, because price is only one cost to the customer. Value is total cost, as the customer uses, acquires, and consumes what he or she buys.

This concept of value represents a melding of two important principles. The first is that value has an essential cost component. We cannot think about value in an economic context without considering cost. The second is that value in a market economy is acknowledged or perceived by the customer. Thus, we must manage our business to satisfy customer requirements with cost-effectiveness. By *cost-effectiveness* we mean that what we supply does any of three things:

1. It reduces cost to the customer.
2. It avoids cost to the customer.

3. It offsets cost by increasing revenue or improving customer cash flow.

This is a powerful rationale for managing a business. It is also a
rationale to which managers and employees can relate.

The Value Network: Back to Basics,
Forward to Fundamentals

In his book *Competitive Advantage*, Michael Porter introduces the
value chain. He describes the value chain as a tool that "disaggre-
gates a firm into its strategically relevant activities in order to
understand the behavior of costs and the existing and potential
sources of differentiation. . . ."[5] A value chain is composed of
generic activities that are linked together to design, produce,
deliver, and support what a business supplies. And in the sense
that these activities must be linked if a business is to gain
competitive advantage, the chain metaphor is meaningful. But
the problem with Porter's view, as I see it, lies first in his notion
of value.

To quote him, "In competitive terms, value is the amount
buyers are willing to pay for what a firm provides them."[6] In
basic economic theory, Porter's definition of *value* is really the
definition of *price*. Price is the amount of money given in exchange
for goods and service. Hence, a competitive price and value are,
by Porter's definition, one and the same thing.

But what about value in use? Buyers buy to use, to consume,
to resell. They buy, and in so doing they incur cost. Do they
receive value when what they buy at a competitive price fails to
meet quality or time requirements? Do they receive value when
what they buy at a competitive price results in excessive costs in
use? Clearly, the answer is no.

A further problem I find with Porter's value chain is that he
views those "strategically relevant activities" in the chain as
functioning in sequential order—inbound logistics, operations,
outbound logistics, marketing, and sales and service. As a tool
for monitoring cost, this sequence makes sense. Inbound logis-

tics—receiving, handling, storing—are the initial activity inputs to cost buildup. Operations, outbound logistics, marketing, and sales and service are subsequent cost adders. But cost adders are not necessarily value adders. And the chain of activities that links cost is truly a cost chain, not a value chain.

But more to the point, value in terms of customer satisfaction and customer cost-effectiveness is not achieved in a linear fashion. It is achieved concurrently and continuously through processes that are integrated by a unifying objective. It is achieved by the meshing of activities and functions through a common strategy. A more appropriate metaphor for describing how value is supplied is a *network*. Hence, a *value network* is an interconnecting web of value-creating and value-adding processes. And we supply value by managing that network for value results.

Recently, I wrote an article for a business publication, which I entitled "Back to Basics." A reader wrote and suggested that it should have been called "Forward to Fundamentals." Whether it's back to basics or forward to fundamentals, we need to rediscover some principles we seem to have forgotten, or principles we've chosen to ignore.

1. Value is acknowledged or perceived by the customer. Value is also relative, so that competition is indeed a factor in the customer's assessment of value.

2. The driving determinant for supplying value is not what customers are willing to pay. It's what we must provide to satisfy customer requirements at least cost of ownership and use. This is not to ignore competitive price, because price is an element of customer cost. But price is only one cost to the customer, and value comprises total cost.

3. We supply value through what we do, what we make, what we sell. We supply value by performing functions and implementing processes that contribute to customer satisfaction and customer cost effectiveness. This is the only measure of value contribution.

4. Activities, functions, and processes entail cost—cost to us the supplier. And that cost is cumulative, recovered profitably

only by a price that generates a margin. But cost adders are not necessarily value adders; and this distinction is not made lightly. Managing a business for cost results is a totally different strategy than managing it for value results. And the customer will be the first to recognize that difference.

5. Managing for value results is managing processes that acquire, create, and add value as we have defined that term. Those processes are interlocked and interwoven in what I call a value network. Processes are made up of functions, so that managing a process demands an understanding of its functions. Managing the value network demands an understanding of all processes and how they interact with each other.

Roadblocks to Managing for Value

Managing for value results is not easy. Indeed, much of what we do in current business practice militates against it. For example:

- We write detailed job descriptions and then classify them into neat categories for wage and salary administration. We rank them in terms of job skill levels, experience, prevailing rates in the area, but definitely not in terms of their contribution to customer satisfaction or customer cost-effectiveness.

- We promote and establish career paths in narrow, functional lines, thereby discouraging cross-functional movement and development. The result is managers who know more and more about less and less, and who lack insights into functions and processes other than their own.

- We identify, accumulate, and allocate cost by product, by function, by department, by calendar time but not in terms of customer value. This gives the highest visibility to internal cost and obscures completely customer requirement and cost concerns.

- We plan, budget, and measure results by cost performance with no relating of cost to value contribution. Whether an activity contributes strongly to customer satisfaction or not at all, we subject it to the same budgetary criteria—percentage of projected income, historical experience, relationship to other activities.

Now clearly, this is not to suggest that we abandon these practices. We must still account for cost and budget for cost performance. And for tax and financial reporting purposes we must conform to accepted cost accounting principles. But to manage for value results we must build in another dimension. We must relate activities and processes to value contribution.

This is a radical reorientation of management perspective. It means redirecting effort and resources from internally driven concerns to external ones. It means thinking about customer satisfaction and customer costs rather than internal considerations and internal cost. It also means looking at the value-supply process as a network of activities that also function in a customer-supplier relationship.

The Makeup of a Value Network

Customers are both external and internal. Obviously those to whom we sell are customers. Indeed, they are the consummate customer. Everything we do is driven by their demands, and value is meaningful only as they acknowledge or perceive it.

But customers are also internal. Activities and processes, within the value network, function in a customer-supplier capacity. Engineering and manufacturing are customers for information and services supplied by marketing. Sales and distribution are customers for products produced by manufacturing. Manufacturing is a customer for materials and services supplied by purchasing. Demands are for results, performance, and information. And a business functions as a true value network when those demands are met reliably and cost-effectively.

The specific activities and processes that make up a value network vary by the nature of the business. A value network for a manufacturer is not the same as that of a health care provider or a wholesale distributor. But all value networks acquire, create, and add value as the customer defines it. The fewer the process steps in identifying and satisfying requirements, the less complex is the value network. Also the fewer the functions to be integrated within those process steps, the less complex is the network.

For example, the value network for retailers like Wal-Mart, Sears, or J. C. Penney is relatively simple. It comprises a marketing and merchandising process that assesses customer demand and determines product mix, inventory levels, and prices to meet that demand. It comprises a value acquisition process that buys from outside suppliers and provides the logistics of receiving, holding, and moving what is bought to the point of sale. It comprises a value-adding process through store operations that not only sell what is bought, but provide customer service after sale. These processes are clear-cut and well defined, and they entail few specialized activities and functions to implement.

When we look at businesses that design, manufacture, market and distribute what they sell, and provide after-sale service and support for what they sell, the value network is more complex. It therefore is more difficult to manage for value results.

Consider manufacturers of computers, telecommunications equipment, and other products that sell through multiple channels. Their value networks certainly comprise a marketing and sales process, but it's complicated by the diversity of the channel and customer mix. Those networks comprise a value-creating design process. But that too is complicated by the multiplicity of engineering functions and disciplines that must be integrated— product engineering, component engineering, materials engineering, reliability engineering, manufacturing engineering, etc.

The same is true for other value-adding processes in these value networks. Procurement and manufacturing include a host of specialized functions—purchasing, inventory control, production scheduling, quality control—and these must all be integrated for value results.

It is this diversity of customer mix and complexity of process and function that make it difficult even to acknowledge a value network, let alone manage it for value results. We're too absorbed in resolving the conflicts these diversities create; too absorbed in the day-to-day crises these complexities generate. And seeking to resolve them solely through "better communication" or by computerizing existing procedures and practices merely obscures the true problem.

To manage for value results we must understand how functions and processes interact, and most importantly, provide a meaningful rationale for them to interact cohesively. That rationale, I submit, is to supply value—to satisfy the requirements of customers, both external and internal, at least total cost of acquisition, ownership, and use.

In the following chapters I will develop the value network concept in greater detail. I will illustrate its application in the value-contributing processes that compose a value network, and demonstrate that application in different business and market environments.

Chapter 2

Management and the Value Network

Networking is one of those terms that has become trendy, even faddish. So it was with some trepidation that I chose the expression *value network*. But as I thought more about the nature of networks, I concluded that this was the best metaphor I could employ to describe how value is created and supplied.

A network is a system of interconnecting elements held together by a unifying design. Network theory is a branch of engineering theory. It's concerned with the characteristics of components, and their interconnection for specific system results.

A typical application of network theory would determine the answers to questions like these: What happens to an electric power distribution system when a short circuit occurs at any point in the system? What are the design requirements of an electrical grid to separate a thousand telephone conversations carried simultaneously on a single cable? What's required at the sending end? What's required at the receiving end? What are the performance and reliability parameters for elements in between?

Network theory is crucial in the design of all complex systems—electrical, mechanical, aeronautical. But we've only begun to understand its application to business systems—systems growing increasingly more complex by exploding technology, market fragmentation, global competitiveness.

Now, this is not a book on network theory. It is a book

developing the concept of value and a book about managing the business for value results.

To achieve those results, we must understand the interconnectivity of processes that create, acquire, and add value as customers acknowledge or perceive it. This interconnectivity is not a straight-line progression of value-adding functional steps. It is not a linear chain of cost-related activities. Rather, it is an intricate and dynamic interweaving of processes and subprocesses, functions and activities, synthesized by a unifying rationale. That rationale, I submit, is the satisfaction of customer requirements cost-effectively. And to manage for that result, we must recognize the network paradigm of that value supply process.

In developing this network thesis, I have used words like *function* and *process*, and these call for some defining. The word *function* comes from the Latin word meaning "to perform" and is defined by *Webster* as "a special duty or performance required in the course of work or activity (the function of an auditor)."[1] And so we refer to an engineering function, a manufacturing function, a marketing function.

The word *process* comes from a Latin word meaning "to proceed" and is defined by *Webster* as "a continuing development involving many changes; a particular method of doing something generally involving a number of steps or operations."

Thus, functions are specific tasks, activities, responsibilities, while processes are continuing means of achieving end results, like designing a product or developing a new market. Functions are particular disciplines, while processes are general approaches to objectives, comprising varying combinations and involvement of functions.

It is this dichotomy of function and process that makes for many of our management problems. Engineering, manufacturing, and marketing are not only functions; more importantly, they are processes. And they are basic processes to the value supply network.

Organizing by Function Is Not Organizing for Value

Formally, we don't establish process networks, least of all networks to supply value. Formally, we organize along functional lines. We make decisions and transmit information through functional channels. We measure, promote, and compensate by functional criteria.

Organizational concepts and practices like these are relics of the past. They developed in an era of large volume, continuous production of standard product, an era of more-stable markets and static technology, an era when suppliers decided what they should produce and markets absorbed what was supplied.

In those days, processes and functions were indistinguishable. The activities of an engineering process were performed exclusively by an engineering function, organizationally entrenched in an engineering department. When engineering was completed, the process of manufacturing began. Drawings and specifications were transferred to a manufacturing function, securely established in a manufacturing department.

Following the planning and scheduling phases of manufacturing, the manufacturing department spelled out purchase requirements, thereby initiating the purchasing process. Requisitions would now be filled by a purchasing function, similarly ensconced in a purchasing department.

And so it went! Or sad to relate, so it still goes!

Though we still organize functionally, we have long understood the shortcomings of that approach. Organizing along functional-departmental lines makes for limited and restricted analysis of risks and opportunities. It promotes the pursuit of functional objectives, often to the detriment of overall business and market concerns. It inhibits cross-functional contact and cooperation and encourages narrow and guarded decision-making.

It is also costly and time-consuming. By establishing functional lines of jurisdiction and information flow, functional structuring creates hierarchies. These are layers of managers and supervisors whose purpose it is to protect functional turf and to facilitate or add to the information flow.

One of our earlier efforts to deal with this problem was matrix management. Here we retained the essentials of the formal, functional structure but added a parallel structure organized along product, project, or program lines. Both structures reported on a solid-line basis to senior management. But functional managers reported also on a dotted-line basis to product, project, or program management.

Thus, a manufacturing manager could report on a solid-line basis to a vice president of operations and on a dotted-line basis to the managers of products A, B, and C. Figure 2-1 illustrates the functional and matrix structures.

Although matrix management models are still employed, the concept has largely gone the route of other management theories. It was publicized, practiced for a time, and then discarded or replaced by something "new."

Of course there was and is a fundamental problem in implementing matrix management. It lies in the dual reporting feature of the concept. It may seem perfectly feasible on paper for managers to report to two different authorities, and be equally responsible and responsive to both. But in the real world, managers act in terms of what they're immediately accountable for, how they are evaluated, and what will directly influence their careers and compensation. This is an understandable behavior mode, but it can prove fatal to matrix management organizations, especially when those organizations are not firmly bound together by some clear and unifying strategy.

The Functional Factor: We Can't Ignore It

More-recent efforts to deal with the problem of functional compartmentalization have proved more successful. Companies have:

- Downsized, eliminating staff and administrative levels that existed largely to coordinate functional activities among multiple plant or operational sites. This has improved communication and information transfer.

- Decentralized along market, product, or technology lines, locating functional activities within division, plant, or business unit structures. This has promoted interfunctional cooperation and speeded up the decision-making process.

- Computerized the gathering, organizing, and disseminat-

Figure 2-1. Functional and matrix organization.

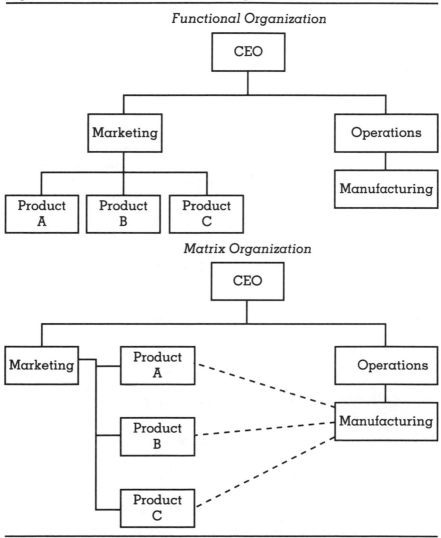

Functional Organization

Matrix Organization

ing of information, thereby surmounting functional barriers and creating databases useful for multifunction applications. This has provided the means to integrate functional activities into larger systems and to capture data on a real-time basis.

- Established formal and informal teams made up of multiple

functional specialists, coordinating their activities for specific goals and objectives. This has rationalized and accelerated the processes of new-product development, quality improvement, capital equipment design and acquisition.

These are all highly desirable developments and in all likelihood they will continue and spread. But all of these developments have a latent weakness, which paradoxically stems from the very factor they were intended to address—the function factor. In seeking to solve the problems of functional compartmentalization, we have gone to the other extreme of ignoring or downgrading the importance of functions.

As I stated earlier, businesses must be managed as process networks; and processes are simply continuous combinations and applications of functions. We cannot manage networks and processes effectively without an understanding of relevant functions: how they interrelate with one another, how they interconnect in larger systems.

The fact is that we are steadily eroding our base of functional expertise and doing little to replace or replenish it.

- By downsizing we have eliminated functional specialists, whose knowledge and experience is gone forever. Within the past few years I have seen dozens of engineering, marketing, and purchasing departments eliminated, with nothing as effective in place to fill the void.

- By decentralizing we have staffed functional activities at operating levels with less experienced and less knowledgeable people. Job classifications and wage and salary structures for functional specialists at those levels cannot attract the talent that was in place at the centralized or corporate level.

- By computerizing databases and information flow, we have provided the means for more-effective management. Too often, however, we lack the functional background to employ those means to full advantage. In a recent *Wall Street Journal* article, Peter Drucker wrote: "Few executives yet know how to ask: 'What information do I need to do my job? When do I need it? In what form? And from whom should I be getting it?' . . . Practically no one asks: 'What information do I owe? To whom? When? In what form?' "[2] Clearly, these questions cannot be answered if we lack functional knowledge and experience.

■ By organizing teams to achieve specific objectives, we have indeed drawn together diverse functional activities. But unless there is functional competence in each activity, and cross-functional understanding among all activities, the team is seriously handicapped. It lacks the ability to see causes and effects, actions and consequences. It lacks the insight to anticipate problems and the foresight to avoid them.

Teams: How and Why They Contribute Value

In their comprehensive study of the global automotive industry, *The Machine That Changed the World*, Womack, Jones, and Roos describe the experience and background of Japanese new-product development teams.

> University trained mechanical, electrical, and materials engineers start their careers in an interesting way . . . they assemble cars.
> At Honda, for example, all entry level engineers spend the first three months in the company working on the assembly line. They're then rotated to the marketing department for the next three months. They spend the next year rotating through the engineering department—drive-train, body, chassis, and process machinery. Finally, after they have been exposed to the entire range of activities involved in designing and making a car, they are ready for an assignment . . . to a new product development team.[3]

We, on the other hand, create teams with engineers having only the slightest understanding of marketing; with marketing people totally ignorant of the engineering disciplines; with manufacturing and purchasing people lacking firsthand experience with both engineering and marketing.

Indeed, we form teams as a morale-building device or as a way of promoting openness and group involvement. We form teams to stimulate some visceral sense of "working together." Under these circumstances, lack of functional knowledge is not too important. In fact, it won't even be recognized.

But if the purpose of a team is what it should be, namely to achieve some specifically identified business objective, lack of functional knowledge is critical. Try reducing the time to market from twenty-four months to six months with a team that is functionally deficient. Or try improving the turnaround time from customer order to delivery from seventy-two to twenty-four hours with a team lacking functional experience and insights. It can't be done.

Successful teams are process networks in miniature. They integrate relevant functions and activities for specified results. They synthesize functional components for team objectives.

But to be successful, teams must be effectively managed. A team leader must coordinate the planning, scheduling, and monitoring of performance. He or she must have access to necessary resources and the authority to employ them as and when needed. Management's failure to provide that limits or even frustrates team success. Too often teams are formed with limited authority. They are led by junior managers, with insufficient clout to command needed people and funding. Or there is no clear directive as to who will lead and channel team effort.

Japanese automotive and electronic manufacturers have been highly successful in employing multifunctional teams. And an important reason for their success is that Japanese manufacturers head up their teams with a strong leader. Toyota pioneered this approach with its shusa system, and Honda with its LPL (large-project leader) system. *Shusa* means simply "the boss." In *The Machine That Changed the World*, the authors describe the difference between team leaders in Japanese and Western (American and European) automotive companies:

> The shusa is . . . the leader of the team whose job it is
> to design and engineer a new product, and get it fully
> into production. In the best Japanese companies, the

position of shusa carries great power and is perhaps the most coveted in the company. . . . Western mass producers also have development team leaders. . . . What's the difference between the two systems? We believe it lies in the power and career path of the team leader. In Western teams, the leader is more properly called a coordinator, whose job it is to convince team members to cooperate. . . .[4]

Since this was written the makeup and power of teams have changed even in the automotive industry. Ford created a self-directing team to design and produce its highly successful Taurus. Development-to-market time was reduced from Ford's normal six years to two years. The General Motors' Saturn division, borrowing from Toyota experience, set up fifteen-member cross-functional teams known as work units. They now provide the model for other GM operations. And Chrysler brought together forty of its most talented engineering and manufacturing specialists, giving them free rein to develop its new Dodge Viper. Despite its $53,000-plus price tag, the 1994 output of this ten-cylinder sports car was sold out in 1993.

In faster-track industries like computers, electronics, and telecommunications, the team approach is more firmly established and more effectively employed.

AN AT&T TEAM reduced the total cycle time on phone-switching computers from a normal time of three years to sixteen months. It reduced manufacturing defects by 87 percent.

A COMPAQ TEAM leapfrogged IBM by designing its new Desk Pro computer around Intel's 386 chip. The time from development to market was an incredible month and a half.

AN NCR TEAM rolled out a new terminal for checkout customers in half the time it normally took for new-product introduction. The terminal has 85 percent fewer parts and can be assembled in half the time of previously designed units.

HEWLETT-PACKARD launched its highly successful Desk Jet printer just twenty-six months after the idea was first considered.

A team of researchers, engineers, and marketers conceptualized the product's design. An enlarged team including sourcing, manufacturing, and software saw the printer through prototype and manufacturing ramp-up.

A MOTOROLA TEAM of high-level engineering and technology specialists developed the production facility for its successful Bravo pager. Interestingly, the Motorola team included a software engineer from Hewlett-Packard.

Teams are most commonly employed to speed up new-product development. The most successful teams and the ones most frequently cited are typically from companies that commercialize advanced technology. They're from companies that seek competitive advantage by introducing more products, to more-specialized market niches, using the latest technology to achieve that result.

But we employ teams to achieve other results. We employ teams to improve product quality. We employ teams to improve customer service. We employ teams to develop and qualify new suppliers and sources. The fact is that long before the team concept became popular we routinely employed teams on a project-by-project basis. At that time, "team leadership" was called project management. Nonetheless, project teams designed and built manufacturing plant and equipment. They designed and built process systems. They designed and implemented information and data systems.

The term *project teams* may not sound as glamorous as new-product development teams, but the requirements for their success are the same. They must be staffed by functionally competent members. They must be tightly focused on specifically defined objectives. They must be managed by team/project leaders having the full support of higher management and the authority to command and employ resources as and where necessary.

There is no question that multifunction teams are the most effective method of integrating disparate disciplines for common objectives. And there is no question that teams are even more effective when they're employed in lean organizations—organizations downsized to remove excess levels of supervision and administration. They become even more effective when companies are decentralized into rational product, market, or business unit operations. They become more effective still when information and accounting systems are better able to identify and track cross-functional processes and activities. We are steadily making progress in all of these areas, but we're still missing a bigger picture.

The Bigger Picture: Setting Company Objectives

Teams are nothing more than microcosms of the network paradigm I discussed earlier. The universe of that microcosm is the business organization as a whole. It is the company, the division, the business unit that epitomizes the essentials of all teams.

Companies are interconnecting webs of processes, functions, and activities. So are teams. Both companies and teams must be managed for defined objectives; both must employ limited resources to achieve those objectives. Our failure to manage the company (the universe) as effectively as we manage the team (the microcosm) is due to the difference in size and scope of the two entities. Every management problem ever experienced by a team is magnified many times over on a company basis.

But more importantly, that failure is due to the lack of company objectives as specific as team objectives. It's due to the lack of objectives clear and compelling enough to synthesize people, processes, and functions; to the lack of objectives flexible enough to guide the company regardless of market or technology changes.

We don't manage companies like successful teams when we set objectives that are merely high-sounding platitudes. It is not a real or compelling objective to strive for "excellence." What does the word mean and how can managers relate to it? So too with an objective like "continuous improvement." What are the standards for measuring current performance, and what are the criteria for measuring improvement? If the standards are merely cost standards, we're fooling ourselves. And if they're not as objective as cost standards, can we effectively manage for so amorphous a goal?

Even goals that have more definite meaning pose problems when they're set as company objectives. The significance may be clear to some but meaningless to others. "Total quality" is one of those objectives. Its meaning is fully understood in manufacturing, purchasing, and logistics. Here *quality* means conformance to specification. But we confuse its meaning when we set total quality management (TQM) as a total company goal. How do you manage for the quality of research and product development? How do you manage for the quality of sales and marketing? Or the quality of any creative or problem-solving process?

Indeed, much of what is assimilated under the umbrella of total quality management is in fact improved customer service, improved responsiveness to customer demands. In engineering, accounting, and other professional service businesses, that would be reducing the costs of client documentation and record-keeping, anticipating problems and advising clients on how best to avoid them, and improving the accuracy and timing of billing.

In manufacturing businesses it would be reducing customer order-processing time, ensuring supply against unplanned usage or premature stockouts. It would be reducing the cycle time from product development to market introduction.

To characterize these objectives as total quality management involves a huge leap from the view of quality as conformance to specification. And in making that leap, TQM enthusiasts dilute the validity and integrity of the quality management concept. By applying it dogmatically across all industry and all process and functional lines, they reduce its credibility. They also promote its being viewed as another fad, rather than a vital and viable objective.

This brings me back to my initial theme. Satisfying customer requirements at least total cost of acquisition, ownership, and use is a clear, definitive, and measurable business objective. It is a powerful yet flexible objective that management can establish to motivate and lead. Creating and supplying value, as customers acknowledge and perceive it, is a rationale fully consistent with the purported objectives of total quality management, continuous improvement, even the pursuit of excellence. But it is a more focused objective, to which every process, function, and activity can relate. It is a sharply defined objective without ambiguity or hyperbole.

Structuring the Value Network: Value-Contributing Processes

To realize the value objective we must manage the business as a value network. As a network, all processes and functions are interrelated. Although each has its own more narrowly defined set of goals, all are integrated by the common objective of customer satisfaction at least cost in use. This is the guiding principle of all effort and activity. It's the rationale for satisfying both the customer to whom we sell and internal customers as well.

In pursuing that objective, we employ processes that create, acquire, and add value as the customer/market acknowledges or perceives it. Although the specific designation of these processes may vary from industry to industry, and the subprocesses and functions they include may vary as well, all value-contributing processes can be grouped under the following five generic headings:

1. *Marketing* is the process that identifies market and customer segments whose requirements are best met through company technology, resources, and capabilities. It is the process that specifies and defines those requirements for subsequent value-contributing processes. Marketing converts customer requirements into customer sales at prices that reflect equitable value in exchange for value given. Marketing administers the sale through final customer acceptance. This may include the physical movement and distribution of finished product through different marketing channels or directly to a user-customer.

Although much has been written and said about its importance, the concept of marketing as a value-creating process is poorly understood. This is particularly true in industrial markets, where the diversity of customer mix and product-service application easily obscures the marketing role in achieving value results.

Industrial markets also tend to be more engineering or manufacturing driven than marketing driven. Marketing's role is better understood in consumer markets, where customer assessments of value are strongly influenced by brand-name imaging, product advertising, and sales promotions. These are more readily seen as value-creating activities.

2. *Engineering* is the process that translates customer requirements into design and performance specifications, usable for internal manufacture or external acquisition. The engineering process combines multiple subprocesses and functions—new-product development, product design, application engineering, process engineering, quality and reliability engineering, manufacturing engineering. In many companies these subprocesses and functions are organizationally fragmented. Some are found in engineering departments; others are found in manufacturing. Often they are located in product, project, or corporate offices.

Regardless of how it is structured, engineering is a value-creating process because it conceptualizes and then details what will satisfy customer requirements. It determines how it should be produced and where—internally or through outside sources.

Engineering for customer value is an integral process, with no barriers between technology and application. It is a continuous process, with no distinction between design and manufacturing. It is a synchronous process, with no time sequencing of one subprocess or one function following another.

This is the meaning of concurrent or simultaneous engineering. And companies like Hewlett-Packard, Intel, AT&T, 3–M, and others who have mastered this discipline give powerful testimony to this value-creating concept of engineering.

3. *Acquisition* is the process of satisfying customer requirements through outside sourcing. Although *purchasing* is the term most often associated with this activity, I prefer *acquisition* to describe the process. Purchasing is more commonly identified with providing materials, equipment, supplies and nontechnical services. Acquisition goes well beyond that. It includes all of the logistics of transporting, storing, and moving purchased materials from source to point of use. It includes the subcontracting of

manufacturing operations and the outsourcing of professional and technical services, data processing, and information systems. Acquisition includes licensing, leasing, partnering, and strategic alliances.

The failure to view acquisition as a value process greatly diminishes a company's effectiveness. It confines management's thinking about customer satisfaction to reliance solely on internal activities and resources. It's like competing with one hand tied behind your back.

The fast-paced computer industry gives ample evidence of this fact. Better than ninety cents on the dollar of product cost on an Apple computer is purchased components and assemblies. Both IBM and Digital Equipment are more vertically integrated, producing more internally and buying less from the outside. Comparative sales and earnings between Apple and IBM and DEC have reflected the consequences of this difference in management philosophy. Recently, both IBM and DEC have reversed course. Both have shut down internal manufacturing facilities and transferred production to outside suppliers and subcontractors.

4. *Manufacturing* is the process that changes the form, configuration, or composition of materials to meet product performance, reliability, and cost requirements. It is a value-adding process that applies labor, equipment, and technology to materials to achieve those results. In so doing it provides a clear example of processes acting in an internal customer-supplier capacity. Manufacturing is a "customer" of the acquisition process. Its requirements are for specified materials, in specified quantities, at scheduled times, to be supplied at lowest cost in use. Manufacturing is a "supplier" to marketing, also for requirements, but requirements specified by external customers.

Although internal customer "requirements" reflect the needs and constraints of specific processes, they must be consistent with the requirements defined by external customers. This explains the manufacturing revolution—some call it deindustrializing—we've been seeing since the turn of the decade.

Large volume, continuous production of standardized product does not satisfy markets today. The demands are for specialized product or product application, produced to rigid quality standards and supplied on order at competitive prices. This calls for small manufacturing units employing flexible manufacturing and modern tool technology to achieve fast turnaround. It calls for greater reliance on outside sources to supply and complement production capabilities. It calls for managing acquisition and manufacturing as two different but complementary value-contributing processes, rather than viewing acquisition as a service or support to manufacturing.

This can be a bitter pill to swallow for those who learned and earned their way in the school of mass production.

5. *Customer service and support* is the process that implements or enhances the value initially sold through services provided after sale. It is a value-confirming and value-adding process that:

- Promotes quick response time from customer order receipt to customer order delivery.
- Ensures complete customer order fill rates with no short fills and no back orders.
- Provides installation, start-up, technical support, and training services to supply full value in use to the customer.
- Replenishes stocks or provides spare parts support to ensure continuous customer availability.
- Provides maintenance and repair services on both a planned and as-needed basis.

Customer service is the process of monitoring customer satisfaction and closing the loop between value sold and value delivered. As such, it demands close meshing with other value-contributing processes in the value network. Yet it is a prime value contributor in its own right. Like acquisition, customer service and support has not been seen in value-contribution terms. Each process has been viewed as an ancillary activity of other processes—acquisition as a service to manufacturing, customer service as a subordinate activity of both manufacturing and marketing.

Given that view of customer service and support, the low

level of customer satisfaction evident in many markets today is not surprising.

Figure 2-2 illustrates the value network, comprising the five value-contributing processes: marketing, engineering, acquisition, manufacturing, customer service and support. All processes are integrated by a common management philosophy. They're bound to a core concept of value as the satisfaction of customer requirements at least cost of acquisition, ownership, and use.

All processes are interconnected, each with every other process. All processes are also impacted by the two external environments with which all businesses must contend—the external demand environment of customers and markets; the external supply environment of suppliers and contractors. The principal factors influencing those environments are:

Figure 2-2. Illustration of the value network.

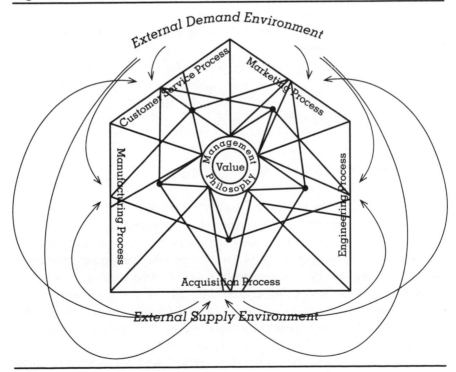

1. Changes in technology
2. The makeup, mix, and volatility of markets
3. The nature and intensity of competition

These environments present opportunities and constraints to the network in producing and supplying value as the customer acknowledges or perceives it. As the environments change, the importance of each process changes in terms of relative value contribution. For example, the rapid pace of technological change in the computer and electronics industries has increased customer demand for new and advanced products and product applications. This has increased the importance of the engineering process in those industries. Since a major source to engineering of advanced technology is outside suppliers, this has also increased the importance of the acquisition process. As the importance of these two processes has increased, the importance of the manufacturing process has declined as a value contributor in the network's ability to meet this changing demand pattern.

It is the task of company management to adjust priorities to reflect significant changes in these external environments, constantly keeping the network focused on fundamental value objectives. It is the task of process management to modify, in lock-step fashion, process objectives to retain the integrity of the network as an effective value-supply system.

Of Course, There Are Other Processes

At this point, I must add a qualifying note. Clearly, there are processes, functions, and activities within a business other than the ones I have described. They are important, and no business could be successful if they were not recognized and managed well. They are the financial, administrative, and human resources activities, basic to all organizations. But they are not value-creating or value-adding activities as I have defined *value*. They don't directly satisfy customer requirements. They don't directly impact customer cost.

This is not to demean these activities and processes, which

play a necessary business role. There is no question that how we manage data processing affects our ability to supply value. So does the managing of our finances. Or the managing of our personnel recruitment, training, and compensation programs. Or, for that matter, the managing of our physical facilities. But these processes and activities are not value-contributing ones, as we have defined that term.

It is of little concern to customers how we perform data processing, or how we administer employee compensation programs, or how we maintain plant and physical facilities. For that matter, it is of little concern to customers whether we actually perform these processes ourselves. Increasingly, companies are outsourcing them, often with more-favorable results than when they were performed internally. Indeed, one of the most reliable criteria for truly effective cost reduction is relating cost of an activity to its value contribution.

If, however, we're in the business of selling outsourced services, like data processing, employee compensation management, or third-party maintenance, it becomes a totally different matter. In that scenario, the processes that provide those services are prime value-contributing ones. They directly satisfy customer requirements. They directly impact customer cost.

This is clearly the case with businesses that design, produce, and market information systems. They're not manufacturers, so for them there is no "manufacturing process" that adds value. Instead there is a system design and development process that employs computer and telecommunications technology to convert data into marketable "products."

This is the business of software companies like Microsoft, Novell, and Lotus. It's the business of systems integrators like Computer Sciences, Anderson Consulting, and Electronic Data Systems. As the lines between product and information become less distinct, the lines between manufacturing and data management processes will become less distinct as well.

However, for the purpose of this book and its thesis of managing for value results, we will concentrate on the five value-contributing processes as we defined them earlier. In the following chapters, we will develop in detail the nature and role of each process.

Chapter 3
Marketing and Value

I never met Sam Walton, but I did correspond with him. What brought this about was an attack on Wal-Mart by the Electronics Representatives Association. The ERA was accusing Wal-Mart of bypassing its members—manufacturers' reps who sell to OEMs and resellers—by buying directly from manufacturers. I wrote an article in a business magazine strongly defending the actions of Wal-Mart. My point was that no one is entitled to business, that everyone must earn it. And if manufacturers' reps provide no values over and above those available from the manufacturer, why shouldn't Wal-Mart buy direct from the manufacturer?

Further, Wal-Mart was merely doing what its customers demanded—supplying brand name merchandise with minimum frills, at low prices. And to do that required the lowest prices from suppliers with no middleman markups added on. Sam Walton read my article and graciously wrote expressing his thanks. He appreciated my "evaluation of the issues" and my comments on his company's "commitment to customers."

The Wal-Mart Story

My relating this incident is in no way intended to readdress those issues. Rather, it is meant to cite a company that understands and practices the principles of value marketing. Wal-Mart, from its very inception, has been tightly focused on the customer and the customer's sense of value. Satisfying customer requirements at lowest cost is a management philosophy that built this company into the $55 billion merchandising giant it is today. That philosophy reflects the deeply held beliefs of the company's founder. It finds reflection today in the people who operate its over 2,000 stores and fifteen distribution centers. It finds clear expression in the company's consistent policy of "everyday low prices," that has resulted in an explosive 30 percent growth even in the recession years of 1991 and 1992.

The key to Wal-Mart's success is its ability to know customer requirements, and satisfy them in as close to real time as possible. The company constantly researches markets to identify and measure customer trends. What are the newest product preferences? What are products of declining interest?

Wal-Mart works with its suppliers to tailor product mix, model variety, and size assortment to meet the needs of each of its store outlets. Through sophisticated inventory management and state-of-the-art computer technology, it continuously shortens the cycle time from customer demand to customer satisfaction. Every sale at a Wal-Mart store is electronically transmitted back to the manufacturer. This instructs the manufacturer on what to ship, when, and how much to schedule for new production.

Commenting in a *Business Week* article on this company-supplier linkage, Wal-Mart's CEO, David Glass, claimed that Wal-Mart was closer to the market and could better define what the customer wanted than the manufacturer.[1] The proof of it lies in the fact that half of Wal-Mart's 5,000 suppliers ask for, and get, point-of-sale data. And the remainder will have to follow suit or cease to be suppliers.

Undoubtedly, Wal-Mart's ability to manage its supply base as effectively as it does is its enormous purchasing leverage. Suppliers—even the biggest of them—are being forced to reassess how they produce, promote, and price their products in terms of how Wal-Mart buys. Wal-Mart's business is too lucrative—and the loss of it too painful—for them not to. But Wal-Mart's leverage derives from its marketing leverage. And that leverage is directly attributable to the effectiveness of its value-driven marketing processes.

In Chapter 2, I described marketing in broad and general terms. It's the process that:

- Targets market segments and identifies customer requirements
- Converts customer requirements into sales at prices consistent with financial, marketing, or other criteria
- Plans, schedules, holds, and moves products from source of supply through sales and distribution channels

In Wal-Mart's case this is a relatively straightforward and clearly defined process. Wal-Mart's market is the mass market for general merchandise ranging from detergents to denims, from coffeemakers to carpet sweepers. Its customers are consumers of brand-name products who seek, first and foremost, ready availability at low prices. These are largely marketing-supplied values. Wal-Mart does not design or manufacture what it sells; it acquires it through purchase. And what and when it purchases, as well as from whom it purchases, are determined solely by the company's assessment of customer demand.

The same is true for Wal-Mart's pricing. Its policy of "everyday low prices" is designed to gain and maintain customer confidence. Wal-Mart's purchasing power gives the company pricing leverage with its suppliers, and the benefits of that leverage it passes on to its customers. Those benefits are not compromised by spontaneous promotions or special sales. Wal-Mart does not believe in them. They are not diluted by shoddy service. Store personnel are committed to prompt and courteous service. Thus, Wal-Mart's merchandising, inventory management, pricing, and store operations are tightly knit together within a value-oriented marketing process that in turn is integrated within an uncomplicated value network. That network is skillfully managed with a clear and compelling strategy. "Everyday low prices" is not only an advertising slogan; it's a management directive.

Value: It's in the Eye of the Beholder

At first glance, it would appear that the Wal-Mart example refutes the notion of value as customer satisfaction at lowest cost of acquisition, ownership, and use. Its operating policy may seem to equate value simply with low price. But low price without available inventory at the point of sale is not value. Nor is low price for products not satisfying customer size, styling, or model needs. Wal-Mart's ability to anticipate customer demand and to supply it as that demand materializes is what creates and adds value over and above low price.

However, where competitive offerings are identical, customers may perceive value solely in terms of low price. This could well be the case where Wal-Mart and K-Mart sell the exact model of a Royal appliance or an exact style of Haggar slacks.

Even where offerings are not the same but the market does not acknowledge a difference, customers may equate value with low price. They do this by ignoring—or failing to see—the differences in product or service features; or they merely assign no consideration to them that might offset a competitive low price.

A classic example of this occurred with Apple Computer in the 1980s. In introducing its Macintosh line, Apple incorporated a number of unique and innovative features—a screen divided into windows, a "mouse," to simplify commands. To punctuate its distinctiveness, Apple put a premium price on the Macintosh. According to John Scully, the company's chairman, this would generate additional revenue and Apple could "then plough some of that back into the market to gain market share."[2]

Unfortunately, the market was not buying a premium price, despite the Mac's unique and innovative features. It was buying IBM PCs or IBM-compatibles. To begin with, most of the software was designed to run on IBM machines. And if the IBM price tag was too high, there were the Dells, Compaqs, and ASTs selling at substantially lower prices. So in the fall of 1990 after six disappointing years, Apple bit the bullet. It drastically cut its prices by 40 percent.

In many respects, Apple's failure with the Macintosh reflected a failure of the company's processes to work as an effective value network. This is particularly true of its marketing process. It was not customer oriented; it was company oriented.

Item

By setting premium prices Apple hoped to generate higher income, and higher income would enable it to gain market share. But this is faulty reasoning. You gain market share by satisfying customer requirements better than competition, by satisfying them more cost-effectively. If you are successful you will experience higher margins, either through larger volume or through higher prices that a satisfied market will now accept. You don't gain market share or experience higher margins merely by raising prices.

Item

Reflecting his Pepsico success with brand management, Scully sought to build an image for the Mac as the "computer for the rest of us." No esoteric, technical jargon. No appealing to the computer eggheads. This was to be a product for the masses. But the masses don't buy computers like they buy soft drinks. Appeals to buy because the Mac is "fun" to use just do not work. A computer is a big investment, and appeals to buy must be more substantive than appeals to having fun.

Item

If Apple were to sell to the masses, it had to have distribution channels that reached them. Those channels would be the large discount retailers, the volume specialty dealers, even the mail-order supply houses. Apple's dealers catered largely to the business community, and the company was slow to franchise dealers in consumer and other nonbusiness markets.

Item

Computers run on software and the most popular software ran on IBM-compatible machines. Apple lacked the capability to develop comparable software internally, and it was not aggressive in acquiring it outside through purchase, license, or strategic alliances. Under the circumstances there was little chance of gaining market share with IBM clones selling at steadily declining prices.

Since those disastrous years, Apple has made a significant turnaround. It has become more price competitive. It has expanded its channels of distribution, selling through retailers, volume specialty stores, and its own mail-order catalogue. The company has greatly expanded its relationships with software and hardware developers, even entering into a joint venture with its once archrival, IBM. This has enabled it to introduce creative new products and product applications in greater volume and at a faster rate. Apple has imposed a tight discipline over product cost by limiting in-house manufacturing to final assembly and buying components and subassemblies on the outside. And its management has become more savvy about the computer market and the customer's perception of value.

Wal-Mart and Apple

It is interesting to compare the Wal-Mart experience with Apple's.

Wal-Mart is in a clearly identifiable market—the retail market for nationally advertised consumer goods. It sells directly to that market through its own company-managed stores. Its sense of value, as customer satisfaction at everyday low prices, is a strong yet credible objective. The company does little or no presale engineering to identify and specify customer requirements. This is done through effective market research and merchandising activity. Customer demand is minimal for after-sale support. The company's value-contributing processes are few, primarily selling and buying, marketing and acquisition. And Wal-Mart's management, from its founder to its leadership, is dedicated to its customer-satisfaction strategy.

Apple, on the other hand, is in multiple markets. It sells through multiple channels—directly to end users and network integrators, and through resellers like distributors and dealers. It designs and manufactures what it sells. Its products satisfy customer requirements only when provided with software systems and programs. And these are developed not only internally but also by outside suppliers.

Apple is in a complex and dynamic business. It straddles computer, electronics, and telecommunications technology. It must be technically innovative and yet price competitive at the same time. This makes for a more complicated value network. It makes for a changing pattern of priority for value-contributing processes.

Lastly, Apple's management, prior to Scully, was not market or customer oriented. Steven Jobs, Apple's founder and first president, was an engineer and his experience in marketing was limited. His interests lay in developing a state-of-the-art personal computer. Notions of customer cost in use were not high on his list of concerns. On the other hand, Scully, Jobs's successor, was a skilled marketing professional. However, his experience was in a different kind of business. Marketing soft drinks and fast food is a far cry from marketing computer and computer-related technology.

Value and the Marketing Concept

It has been almost two decades since Theodore Levitt's "Marketing Myopia" appeared in the *Harvard Business Review*. And with that article there evolved the marketing concept, the idea that business must be a customer-satisfying process rather than a product-producing one.[3]

The marketing concept found ready acceptance in consumer-goods business. Here, the customer was an individual, with tastes and preferences that not only could be measured but influenced through advertising, brand-name imaging, and promotional sales. Products could be easily introduced, convincingly labeled, or even replaced by new products as customer demands changed. And this could all happen using the same technology, facilities, and production processes. So whether a company sold bleaching powder A or super bleaching powder B made little difference. Marketing—comprising advertising, promotion, sales, and distribution functions—could still work as a fully integrated process. And orienting that process to the customer, rather than to the product, was a relatively easy adjustment. Indeed, as the marketing concept spread, it became a necessary adjustment because competition imposed it.

In industrial markets the marketing concept has either been ignored or poorly understood. Certainly it is badly implemented. Too often, it's seen merely as a matter of organizing related functions into a marketing department. Or employing statistical models, borrowed from consumer-goods applications, to simulate market behavior. These are faulty or simplistic notions.

Marketing in the industrial arena is a value-creating process that:

- Identifies and defines customer requirements
- Translates product, service, technology, and resource capabilities into customer-satisfying offerings
- Negotiates prices providing value in exchange commensurate with value supplied
- Establishes and administers channels of distribution to targeted market segments
- Provides before-sale and after-sale service and support to ensure customer satisfaction

Marketing is the process that gives direction and focus to all other processes. It is the process that guides all functions and activities in satisfying customer requirements cost effectively.

Who Is the Customer, and What Are Customer Requirements?

Identifying customer requirements is the first step in the marketing process. In consumer-goods business this is done through market research, focus group surveys, demographic analysis, historical projections of buying patterns and trends. These involve statistical techniques, some of them extremely sophisticated. But the process is tried and proven. And it is reasonably effective. The consumer market is a mass market and statistical analysis provides meaningful data on customer wants and preferences.

Identifying customer requirements becomes more difficult the more removed the business is from consumer-product markets. First of all, there is the question of who is the customer. In consumer markets it is the individual at the store counter or at the gasoline pump with the full power to make a buying decision. In industrial markets the customer is rarely a single individual. Rather, it is a mix of individuals—I call them buying influences— performing different functions and with different perceptions of requirements and value. There are those who specify; those who select sources; those who negotiate agreements; those who finance, operate, or maintain what is bought. There is higher management. Who is the customer?

Again, in industrial markets customers buy in different buying capacities. They buy as end users to use or consume what they buy. They buy as OEMs to incorporate what they buy into what they sell. They buy as resellers, who sell to distributors and dealers, who in turn sell to end users and OEMs. A producer of pumps, valves, motors, or bearings could easily be selling in all markets at one and the same time. Who is the customer, and what are customer requirements?

The problem becomes increasingly more difficult in industries where technology is expanding. As technology changes, markets change, and as markets change, requirements change. Less than a dozen years ago both Microsoft and Intel were newly developed suppliers to industry-dominant IBM. Microsoft supplied software to its IBM-OEM customer. Intel supplied microprocessors to be employed as components in IBM machines.

Today, technology has made computers commodities. The real value is added through software and microchip technology. IBM has become just another channel of distribution for Microsoft and Intel products. Indeed, both companies are now directing their marketing efforts at large company end users. Industry analysts report that Microsoft has set up "evangelist teams" to cultivate new users in fields such as finance, government, and health care. Intel has assembled a team of one hundred "architecture managers" to convince corporations that Intel microprocessors will satisfy more than their PC needs. From being strictly suppliers to OEMs and distributors, Microsoft and Intel are now developing into suppliers to the end-user market.

Requirements Are "Derived"

Customer requirements in industrial, commercial, and institutional markets are derived requirements. They flow from the demands and constraints imposed on customers by the products they produce, the processes they perform. The demand for automobiles, kitchen appliances, and building construction is what creates requirements for steel. The demand for manufacturing efficiency is what constrains the continued use of energy wasteful equipment.

Derived demands flow from competition and the marketplace. Competitive pressures for lower prices create requirements for lower-cost manufacturing through outside contractors. Market demands for new or improved products constrain producing and marketing products with declining appeal.

Marketing value begins with knowing the customer's business and knowing it in detail. In many cases, this means knowing the customer's customers' business. What drives purchase requirements? What constrains them? Figure 3-1 is an illustration adapted from my earlier book *Value Selling*. It shows the relationship between derived or imposed demands and requirements by type of customer—reseller, OEM, and end user. For example, the demands imposed on end users are essentially process demands. They reflect problems and opportunities like:

- Inability to control quality
- Inadequate capacity to handle production and sales volume
- Inadequate control of waste or hazardous materials

Purchase requirements of the end user therefore are for machinery and equipment, laboratory and test facilities, technical and professional services, data-processing systems and software. And important buying influences are specifiers, users, and higher management.

Figure 3-1. Determining requirements by customer type.

Type of Customer	Interprets	Imposed Demands	Defines	Requirements
Reseller	→	*Market and competitive demands* for price, quantity/time, after-sale service and support performance *Process demands*—marketing and distribution, finance and administrative processes	→	*Commodities*—products he or she buys and resells *Commodities*—standard equipment, operating supplies; *systems* and *services*
Original equipment manufacturer (OEM)	→	*Market and competitive demands* (same as for reseller) *Product demands*—for design, performance, reliability *Process demands*—manufacturing, engineering, procurement, marketing and distribution, finance and administration	→	*Commodities*—raw materials; standard parts and components; operating, repair, maintenance, office supplies *Specialty items*—parts, assemblies made to customer design *Services*—manufacturing engineering, financial, et al. *Systems*—in all areas
End user	→	*Process demands*—manufacturing, engineering, distribution, finance and administration	→	*Commodities*—maintenance, repair, operating and office supplies *Services*—specialized and professional *Systems*—in all areas

Source: Adapted from Louis J. De Rose, *Value Selling* (New York: AMACOM, 1989).

The demands imposed on resellers are largely market and competitive demands. They reflect the fact that resellers provide a logistical and financial function in the markets they serve. They carry the range and mix of products that customers are not willing or able to carry. They supply product in customer-convenient quantities and frequency, at favorable terms of payment. And they must sell at competitive prices. Their purchase requirements, therefore, are for:

- Products that are compatible with other products they sell
- Products that already have market acceptance
- Quantities and delivery schedules that enable them to meet the pattern of their customer demands
- Attractive prices with favorable terms of payment

The most important buying influences on resale customers are higher management, marketing and financial management.

The demands imposed on OEM customers are product, technology, and competitive demands. They reflect the demands of the OEM market for product performance and reliability, adequate supply to satisfy demand, and assured after-sales service. Purchase requirements are for materials, components, and services that go into the products OEM customers produce. They are for conformance to quality specifications. They are for quantities and delivery dates capable of meeting manufacturing schedules. They are also for competitive prices. On critical application materials and components, primary buying influences are specifiers in product and design engineering. On commodity-type materials, purchasing managers and buyers are important buying influences.

The challenge to marketing in creating value, therefore, is twofold. It must:

1. *Identify specific customer requirements in detailed technical, logistics, and cost terms.* It does this by segmenting markets into tightly defined buying arenas by technology, application, customer size, buying influence, geography, and other relevant criteria.

2. *Translate customer requirements internally to other value-contributing processes* through meaningful product, performance, and cost specifications. The aim is to ensure an ideal fit between customer demand and supplier capabilities and resources.

The task of achieving this twofold objective is that of the product-planning and pricing functions of the marketing process.

Product Planning: IBM and Motorola

Planning and developing product and product applications tends to be either internally or externally oriented. Too often it is the former. We develop products around existing designs, utilizing existing manufacturing methods and processes. The reasoning is "Don't fix what ain't broke." If we've been successful marketing the product in the past, why change? If we've invested in facilities and know how to produce that product, why not use them to the fullest?

The problem with this kind of reasoning is that it's badly focused. It looks to internal concerns, not to market realities. It ignores changes in technology and changes in market behavior that are the prime determinants of what we should produce, what we should supply.

The drastic decline of IBM from its once lofty position in the computer industry provides a dramatic example of product planning that was badly focused. For years, IBM had prospered by pursuing a strategy based on its big mainframe computers. Selling a mainframe meant selling IBM operating systems, IBM storage and processing devices, IBM software and applications. Selling an IBM mainframe meant creating a continuing, captive market for additional IBM products and services.

All this changed in the 1980s when minicomputers and personal computers took off. Silicon chips and computer components became standardized, allowing dozens of companies to design and build around standard computer platforms. This was the breakthrough to "open architecture," bringing to an end

IBM's captive hold on systems design and application. The explosive growth of the PC market stimulated the development of more-powerful and -versatile components and software. Soon, PCs were attaining the performance levels previously achieved only by large mainframe computers; and the days of IBM dominance were over.

In sharp contrast with IBM's approach to market and product planning is that of Motorola. From its founding in the late 1920s, Motorola has developed into a fine art the talent for predicting changes in customer demand. The company started with car radios and from that beginning branched out into two-way radios and television. Anticipating the revolution in microelectronics, Motorola moved into integrated circuits and semiconductors. At the same time it got out of the television business, selling its Quasar line to Matsushita Electronics of Japan. Motorola decided that to be successful it had to surpass Japanese electronic manufacturers in performance and cost to the customer. As a result the company invested billions in redesigning phones and pagers to be simpler, smaller, lighter, and defect-free. Today, the company dominates the cellular phone and pager market, not only in the U.S. but in Japan.

For years, Motorola has maintained an "intelligence department" with the directive to report on the latest technology developments. The information developed by that department is circulated in what the *Wall Street Journal* calls "intelligence road maps."[4] These keep the company abreast of technology breakthroughs and assess their potential for new product development. They project customer demand, time-to-market, and comparative costs, both for Motorola and expected competitors. These road maps are what give direction to the company's marketing and other processes. They are what integrate those processes into a value network supplying what the company calls "total customer satisfaction."

Comparing the IBM and Motorola experiences in three areas highlights the differences in market and product planning between the two:

1. Although the scope and caliber of IBM's technology is

second to none, the application of it to new-product development is diffused. There are—or have been—too many layers of bureaucracy within the company hierarchy, too many competing interests to give that research clear direction. Motorola, on the other hand, is more clearly focused. Its aim is total customer satisfaction and all market research and product development is fixed on that objective. Lesson number 1 therefore is that product planning must be market and customer focused.

2. IBM's commitment to its mainframe strategy strongly influenced its development in minicomputers, PC microprocessors, drives, and storage devices. Engineering, manufacturing, and acquisition resources supported this marketing strategy, although technology and the marketplace were making it obsolete. Motorola, on the other hand, was not blindsided by any such commitment. When margins were first threatened by Japanese price competition, the company sold its television business. When cellular phones first showed the potential for becoming the communication wave of the future, Motorola invested billions in receiving and transmitting products and systems. Lesson number 2 therefore is that market and product planning, though focused, must not be locked into preconceived business and market strategies. It must be flexible and adaptable to changing technical and economic environments.

3. IBM, rightly or wrongly, developed a reputation for being arbitrary, if not arrogant. By pursuing its mainframe strategy, it often appeared to be pushing product rather than solving customer problems cost-effectively. Motorola, on the other hand, has shown an acute awareness of customer costs. Its cellular phones contain 70 percent fewer parts than its competitors' and are virtually defect free. The company is dedicated to reducing its manufacturing defect rate by 90 percent every two years, and its cycle time for new-product introduction by 90 percent every five years. Lesson number 3 is that market and product planning, like all value contributing activities, must aim for customer cost reduction or customer cost containment.

Value Pricing

Like product development, pricing can also be internally or externally oriented. It is internally oriented when the objective of price is to recover cost as it is experienced or projected. Or, it is to allow for a margin above cost as some return on investment or return on sales. Although recovery of cost and profit are necessary business objectives, they are strictly internal considerations. They are of little concern to customers and markets.

Even pricing that is externally oriented may be poorly directed. Pricing to competition is an improvement over pricing from cost, because it drives all processes and functions to meet the competitive challenge. But it is still is not customer oriented.

Value pricing is pricing that quantifies value as it is acknowledged or perceived by the customer. What is the worth to the customer in dollars and cents to have requirements satisfied by our product and service offerings? How does what we supply reduce cost in use, avoid it, or offset it by increasing revenue or improving customer cash flow? How do these cost benefits, together with the price we propose, affect total cost to the customer? These are the questions we must address if we are to do value pricing. These questions do not ignore cost and profit concerns or competitive considerations. They simply complement them.

Value pricing is a relatively new approach to pricing. In industries where it is employed, it is sometimes known as "yield management." The concept recognizes that the same product or service satisfies customer requirements differently. It also impacts costs of acquisition, ownership, and use differently. Therefore, by grouping customers into common categories of requirements-satisfaction and cost-effect, marketers can now price to enhance their revenue, improve their yield. Following are common examples of this pricing approach:

GAS, ELECTRIC, AND WATER UTILITIES offer different rates to different customers—government, institutional, large industrial, small industrial, commercial, and residential. They also offer different rates for peak-hour and slack-hour consumption and for seasonal demand.

AIRLINES recognize that travel requirements are more urgent for business people than they are for non–business people. They also recognize that non–business travelers have more flexibility on schedules and being away from home. Thus, airlines set higher fares for midweek travel and for midday flights.

RADIO AND TELEVISION BROADCASTERS, HOTELS AND RENTAL CAR FIRMS know there are high-demand and low-demand times for their offerings. Rates for radio and TV prime time—7 to 10 P.M.—are considerably higher than those for midday or for after midnight.

In an innovative approach, Procter and Gamble has initiated what it calls value pricing by selling at uniform prices. Historically, producers of consumer goods have sold to the large supermarket chains with price discounts, rebates, and advertising and trade allowances. This has led to overstocking by some stores to take advantage of price concessions, and inventory stock-outs at stores unwilling or unable to buy in larger volume.

The practice of promotional sales and discount prices has also led to bargain hunting by supermarket customers—P&G's channel to the ultimate market. The company is convinced that brand loyalty suffers when prices fluctuate widely from store to store, and it suffers also when store inventories are not ensured. As a consequence, Procter and Gamble has reduced prices on more than half of its brand name products, some of them by as much as 25 percent, and eliminated promotion subsidies and discounts.

It is interesting to note that P&G's "everyday low price" is precisely the strategy—even the terminology—employed by Wal-Mart. Both are customer oriented: Wal-Mart to the value perceptions of the consumer, P&G to that same consumer but through its immediate customer Wal-Mart. It is also interesting to note that Wal-Mart's purchases account for 11 percent of P&G's sales.

Industrial Markets and Value Pricing

Yield management—or value pricing—in the industries cited is relatively easy to employ. Customer segments are readily identifiable. Their demand for product or service is highly elastic with changes in price. Costs of producing or supplying are not a direct function of customer quantities. Rather, they are more-fixed or average costs experienced over total business volume. Thus, the significant factor in pricing is the market's sensitivity to price change, customer segment by customer segment.

Where products are purchased to customer specification or tailored to meet unique customer application, value pricing, as yield management, is more difficult to employ. Customers are not easily segmented into distinct and precise buying categories. Costs of production tend to be a direct function of each customer's requirement rather than fixed or average costs. Hence, in industrial markets it is common for pricing to be cost-based pricing. Or, it is pricing to meet competition. Neither of these, however, is customer-oriented pricing; neither of these is value pricing. Nonetheless, value pricing is a realistic and viable approach to pricing even in industrial markets.

I recently saw a striking example of value pricing in the machine tool industry. The transaction involved the production of process equipment to meet customer design, performance, and maintenance requirements. The equipment was being purchased to replace aging machinery that was inefficient, costly to operate and maintain, and incapable of satisfying quality and production demands.

In discussions with the customer's engineering and manufacturing people, the supplier gained information on customer cost and operating experience with the existing equipment. By detailed cost analysis, it estimated that its equipment's design and performance would reduce the cost of quality failure by a minimum of 15 percent. It would reduce the cost of manufacturing and maintenance labor by 20 to 25 percent. It would increase inventory turnover rates from the current four times per year to ten, thereby reducing the cost of capital by 18 to 20 percent. The supplier annualized these reductions and avoidances over five years, which was the time the customer used as the investment payback period.

Based on its analysis, the supplier quoted a price representing half of the projected five-year savings. This was higher than its estimates of cost plus profit markup, and substantially higher than expected competitive prices. Admittedly, the supplier was a preferred source, selected for negotiation on the basis of technical evaluation. But the supplier was also confident that the price it quoted was fully supportable. The bottom line was that the customer received a price that quantified value in use. And the supplier received a price that was value in exchange commensurate with value supplied. That's value pricing.

Value Selling: Sales, Distribution, and Advertising

Market segmenting, product planning, and pricing are the strategic activities of value marketing. They provide the guidance to other functions within the marketing process. They provide the focus and direction to other value-contributing processes within the value network.

Sales, advertising, and distribution are the functions that implement the value marketing strategy. Sales creates value by generating customer acknowledgment of value supplied. Advertising creates value by stimulating market perceptions of value offered. Distribution creates value by satisfying customer requirements for product availability at the point of purchase. It adds value by providing cost-effective services that enhance product value. In the context of value marketing, I group sales and advertising together, because they are both facets of what I call *value selling*. Value selling is the subprocess within marketing that develops customer interest, translates offerings into customer benefits, and effects the sale.

Value selling through sales is selling through people. They may be organized in a sales department, a product, an application, or a geographical sales office. They may be single individuals or organized in selling teams. They may be inside salespeople selling via telephone contact or field salespeople dealing with customers on a face-to-face basis.

Value selling through advertising is selling through the media. It's selling through the written or spoken word, through photography, artwork, graphics. In consumer markets, advertising develops brand identification and promotes brand loyalty. It presells products long before an actual sale. Advertising can do this because consumers buy to satisfy wants as well as needs. They buy for personal reasons. These are emotional; they are psychological. So appeals to beauty, health, security, adventure are highly effective in influencing sales. In consumer markets, customers perceive value in the message and images that advertising projects. Or they acknowledge it in the "everyday low prices" that advertising proclaims.

Industrial, commercial, and institutional buyers do not buy for personal reasons. They buy to satisfy requirements that are driven by technical, economic, and cost demands. They are driven by market and competitive forces. Selling value in these markets—either through personal sales or advertising—is not a play on emotions. It is a planned and disciplined process that:

1. *Identifies who in the customer organization is a meaningful buying influence.* Buying influences are those with the authority to make or affect buying decisions. Value selling targets them in terms of interest and concerns, their sense of requirement and value.

2. *Proposes solutions to specific problems and opportunities as seen by buying influences.* What is a problem or solution to a problem may be seen differently by a buying influence who specifies requirements as against one who must use or operate what is specified. Value selling tailors the message to the perception of specific buying influences.

3. *Translates product and service features into benefits that satisfy customer requirements.* If the requirement is to reduce scrap loss, what design or performance features in our product offering achieve that result? If the requirement is faster and more reliable replenishment of customer inventories, what stocking and shipping services do we provide to ensure that?

4. *Quantifies benefits into cost-effective terms.* When we demonstrate how our offering reduces scrap or speeds up inventory replenishment, what is the impact on customer cost? How does it reduce customer cost? By how much? How does it avoid customer cost? By how much? How does it offset customer cost by increasing revenue or improving cash flow? By how much and over how long a period of time?

In my earlier book, *Value Selling* (AMACOM, 1989), I developed the concept and techniques of value selling in considerable detail. The book reflects years of consulting and training experience with dozens of companies in a wide spectrum of industry. What prompted it was my conviction that too few companies understood and practiced value selling. They did product selling—that is, they sold product features, not benefits. And if they sold benefits, they failed to translate them into customer cost terms. Failing to sell on the basis of customer cost necessarily means selling on the basis of competitive price. And without undisputed cost leadership, that's a dangerous strategy to follow.

One company that is most effective in value selling is General Electric. For years it has trained its salespeople to know the customer's business, to understand value and how costs cluster, and to translate product and service features into cost-effective solutions.

I had the opportunity of presenting value-negotiation workshops for GE's Apparatus Sales, and was impressed with the knowledge and skill GE sales engineers displayed. They were well versed on how cost behaved—fixed costs, variable costs, costs of capital. They understood return on investment and return on assets principles. They could factor cost improvements into customer-employed formulations to justify prices even when they were higher than competition. There is little question in my mind that a major reason for GE's continuing success is its superiority over competition in selling value to diverse markets.

Another highly successful company that has mastered the principles of value selling is National Starch and Chemical. A highly profitable subsidiary of Unilever—one of the world's largest producers of packaged consumer goods—NSC maintains a low profile. But its salespeople are well trained in communicating value as the customer perceives it. NSC salespeople "must be able to verbalize and quantify unique value added characteristics of [their] products in terms familiar to the customer—in terms of customer cost."[5] They must be able to quantify "value in use." In developing sales presentations NSC salespeople go through a disciplined analysis of:

- Customer costs of production
- Contributing costs of NSC materials
- Key value contribution of NSC materials to the satisfaction of customer requirements
- Effect of that contribution on customer costs in use

This analysis is adjusted for the number of production lines the customer operates, the number of shifts per day, the number of hours per week, month, and year. This approach to customer cost is what enables the company to be a preferred supplier and to avoid selling at simple competitive low prices.

Advertising: Where the Message Is Not Always the Message

Although advertising is another form of selling, it's distressing how poorly value selling principles have found expression in advertising copy. This is particularly true in industrial and commercial markets. Too often the appeals in these markets are empty and inane. "Invest in the future," "Get a warm feeling inside," "Experience a dream." These are real ads; I'm not making them up. And more to the point, they're more the rule than the exception.

One outstanding exception was a Texas Instruments advertisement entitled "Texas Instruments Reveals Why Savvy OEM's Distinguish Between Semiconductor Price and Total Cost of Ownership."[6] The Texas Instruments advertisement appeared in design engineering and electronic publications, purchasing and materials management magazines, and business journals. In so doing, it addressed its message to key buying influences.

The advertisement spoke of TI world-class manufacturing excellence that assured major customers of "ship-to-stock" delivery, avoiding the expense of all incoming inspection. It spoke of major advances in computer-aided design tools and manufacturing processes that enabled TI to achieve near-perfect quality and reliability. It described product and service features that met customer purchase requirements. Lastly, the advertisement related features to customer cost. It identified what it called cost culprits, the "areas where total costs of ownership can result and which TI semiconductors could reduce or avoid." These were:

1. *Incoming inspection*—uncertain quality requires 100 percent inspection of incoming devices. Cost-of-ownership adder: $0.10.
2. *Inventory*—undependable deliveries require a maintenance and warehousing of backup stocks. Cost-of-ownership adder: $0.12.
3. *Systems manufacturing*—high IC failure rates require 100 percent component burn-in plus systems rework. Cost-of-ownership adder: $0.24.
4. *OEM warranty*—poor IC reliability results directly in increasing costs of honoring warranties. Cost-of-ownership adder: $0.53.
5. *End-user maintenance*—costs are incurred to keep systems operational in the field. Cost-of-ownership adder: $1.06.

By asking its readers to factor in these "cost culprits"—the cost-of-ownership adders—the advertisement asked readers to compare TI to competitive offerings on a total cost of ownership basis. This is a succinct but effective value-selling message.

Value in Distribution

Distribution is the subprocess of marketing that closes one loop between sales and customer satisfaction. It delivers what sales has sold.

Distribution is a value-adding activity when it meets consumer requirements for time, place, and utility benefits cost-
effectively. This means supplying the specified mix and quantity
of product at the customer's point of use, in the shortest time, at
the lowest total cost. Necessarily, this can occur only when
distribution is integrated with other marketing activities, and
integrated further with all value-contributing processes within
the value network.

In theory, this integration is easier when manufacturers sell
and distribute their product directly. There are no intermediaries
between the producer and the consumer to interfere with the
communication flow. There are no middlemen whose interests
and objectives the manufacturer will have to consider.

However, this can be illusory. In today's technical and economic environment, this can be a handicap rather than an advantage. Having no intermediaries between producer and consumer
limits the scope and diversity of the manufacturer's market. It
cannot cover all bases, nor cover the ones it does effectively. Also,
it can receive false signals as to market demand, product acceptance, and competition, which false signals will misdirect all other
activities and processes.

Accordingly, the trend is increasingly to market through
outside channels. For all products, the percentage of products
sold through outside distribution has gone up from 20 percent in
1980 to 30 percent in 1990, and is climbing rapidly.[7] This development is most pronounced in industries with rapid technological change and volatile markets. These are factors that increase
the manufacturer's risk of creating and holding inventories, and
marketing through independent resellers is one way of reducing
risk.

The computer and electronics industries are clear illustrations
of where this is happening. Indeed, it's happening at such a rate
that it's creating a whole new set of marketing problems. Manufacturers are setting up marketing channels that overlap and often
compete with each other—distributors, dealers, aggregators,
value-added resellers, super stores, mail-order houses. At the
same time they also sell and ship direct. This complicates the task
of integrating distribution with product planning, pricing, sales,

and advertising. It greatly complicates the task of integrating it with other functions and processes.

It is essential to recognize that independent channels are integral elements of the marketing process. They complement the manufacturer's sales and distribution capabilities. They are important value adders. They are not "customers" to be sold to. They are partners in satisfying the ultimate customer—the end user and the OEM.

Manufacturers should employ channels to supply values they cannot supply as well, or to add value over and above product values. The same strategic analysis that identifies market segments in which to compete, is what's required in the selection of distribution channels. It assesses and defines:

- The ultimate customer base to be served and the number of channels required to serve it well
- The functions that each level must be capable of performing to satisfy customer requirements—application engineering, promotion, physical distribution, financing
- How distribution flows of information, order processing, technical support, payments, returns are to be managed—forward to the ultimate customer, backward to marketing and other processes

Companies that do this well are the 3M Company, Allen-Bradley, and AMP. By careful evaluation of their end-customer base and the capabilities of channels to serve them, all three have built up powerful distribution systems. Their thrust is customer satisfaction, and they rely heavily on independent distributors to achieve it.

Increasingly, these companies are pushing the customer interface outward to distributors who can provide value-added services—services that were once the domain of the manufacturer and/or the customer. By centralizing warehouses and pursuing economies of scale their distributors are better able to satisfy end-customer demands. Meanwhile, all three manufacturers are decentralizing warehousing and pursuing the just-in-time initiative with key customer accounts.

It is interesting to note that out of fifty-five electronics distributors, between a quarter and a third now supply value-added services that were once performed either by the manufacturer or the customer.[8] These include customer assembly and testing, kitting, in-plant stores, special packaging, wire stripping and striping, bar coding, free technical support, and flexible financing.

It is safe to say that companies that fail to provide value-added distribution, either directly or through independent channels, are doomed to failure. In the electronics industry alone, at least twenty distributors have gone out of business in the past decade. In other industries—like steel, machinery and equipment, and manufacturing supplies—a similar pattern is developing. The reasons for failure are either the inability to see the evolving trend to value-added distribution, or the lack of resources to implement it.

Steve Menefee, president of Arrow/Schweber, one of the leading distributors in the electronics industry, notes that distribution is a business "where size and economies of scale offer distinct benefits to the customer."[9] Arrow consolidates a $300 million inventory into four computerized, automated distribution centers. It has lowered the cost of storage and distribution while establishing on-time delivery and quality standards that *Electronic Buyers News* has found led the industry.[10] It has extended its value-added approach to distribution by expanding its turnkey or contract manufacturing activities. This is a service in which the distributor handles everything from design to delivery of completely assembled circuit boards. According to Menefee this is the fastest growing segment of the distribution business.

The increased power and sophistication of industrial customers, driven by complex technical and economic change, are drastically altering distribution as an element of the marketing process. Manufacturers are reducing their sales force and concentrating on a smaller number of large-volume customers. They are producing on a just-in-time basis for those customers; carrying inventories to support their future demands; even consigning inventory to them to be paid for only when used. Manufacturers are supplying product as "ship to stock," which means at assured quality levels, with no incoming inspection required. They are providing special features of product or package design that permit easier, quicker, safer handling, movement, and use. Continuously, the aim is customer satisfaction at lower cost.

For other than the large-volume end users and OEMs, manufacturers are relying on independent distributors—independent, however, only in the sense that they are not manufacturer owned. Distributors are channels in the marketing process. And as such they must be integrated with all other functions in that process. This means developing common strategies, identifying and sharing responsibilities, promoting open exchange of information, and establishing relationships of loyalty and cooperation. Most of all it means a common dedication to customer value.

To paraphrase the Chrysler advertisement, in marketing value through distribution "you lead, you follow, or you get out of the way."

Chapter 4

Value and the Engineering Process

Engineering is the application of scientific knowledge to practical use. As a value-creating, value-contributing process, it applies that knowledge to satisfying customer requirements cost-effectively. Although this is a concept readily understandable in theory, in practice it is difficult to realize. Two factors account for this:

1. Our structuring of engineering tasks along functional lines, and departmentalizing them into narrow fields of specialty
2. The explosive growth of scientific knowledge and that body of knowledge we call technology

I touched on the first factor in Chapter 2. Since the days of Frederick Taylor in the early 1900s until only recently, the accepted wisdom has been to break down tasks into their smallest components and then tackle them sequentially. This is the reasoning behind the mass production line, and that same reasoning lies behind much of what we do in engineering.

Taylor's precepts, and their expression in mass production manufacturing, espoused also the benefits of vertical integration, that is, supplying internally everything from the final product back to the basic materials going into that product. Thus, an early

Ford Motor not only assembled automobiles; it produced subassemblies, parts, and even the steel, rubber, and glass from which those parts were fabricated.

So too, engineering in much of our industry is vertically integrated. It begins with engineering research and continues through advanced design, product design, process engineering, production engineering, and quality control. It encompasses everything from material and component engineering to engineering for performance or product characteristics, to engineering for reliability, manufacturability, and maintainability.

These tasks are performed in some chronological or causal fashion: component engineering following product design, quality engineering following design evaluation. They are performed in separate divisions, departments, sections, and branches, each having its own hierarchy and each its own reason for being.

This approach to engineering finds its most extreme expression in missiles and aerospace, military aircraft and electronics, and other weapons systems–type industry. It prevails because government procurement policies and practices multiply enormously the engineering workload. They do this by:

- Imposing specifications and standards on materials, processes, and test and inspection procedures that would not be required in commercial production
- Promoting competitive sourcing, through government purchase specifications, rather than relying on commercially identifiable parts and components (Witness the nine pages of government-required specifications for a simple glass ashtray cited in Vice President Gore's study on restructuring government.)
- Requiring detailed drawings, specifications, test results, source justifications, and documentation covering even the minutest element of engineering activity

Many of these requirements are spelled out as specification or work-scope items. And since most if not all of these tasks are allowable costs under government contracts, management accepts and justifies their performance. The consequence is that the engineering process in defense industry is overstaffed, overspecialized, and overcontrolled. It is not an integrated process of value-contributing functions. It is not integrated with other processes in any discernible value network.

Admittedly, military and defense industry is not representative of all industry. But to some degree, most industries still divide the engineering process into separate functional organizations, with separate functional criteria for their performance.

Often, however, those criteria conflict. What may be deemed excellence in design engineering could well result in headaches for production engineering. The stories are legion of product engineering designing products with no knowledge of whether manufacturing equipment and tooling could produce them reliably, or whether they would be manufactured internally or supplied by outside contractors.

The problems thus created are magnified by the second factor I cited. As scientific discoveries develop new bodies of knowledge, engineering tasks become more complex. As technology—the application of that knowledge—expands, those tasks become more specialized. The result is a growing intellectual gap between one engineering discipline and another, and uncoordinated effort among all disciplines. Design engineers, for example, don't speak with manufacturing engineers in the same language. Too often, they don't speak at all.

A company with which I have consulted, and whose engineering skills I have come to respect, is the Timken Company. As a world leader in bearings and steel for bearings, Timken is familiar with the problems I have just described. R. L. Leibensperger, Timken's vice president of technology, puts it in the following terms:

> The engineer, burdened with technology overload, has had to focus on increasingly more specific areas of expertise. Management too, faced with global competitive pressures, has forced the engineer into a short-term problem-solving mode. . . . The significant gains made by process engineers due to precision manufacturing often go unnoticed by his product engineering counter-

part. Thus, while design engineers are using today's state-of-the-art computer tools to design their products, they are often using material constants and property characteristics in their design algorithms that represent 1950's standards.[1]

It's as if one part of an orchestra is playing one melody, and the other part is playing another, while the conductor is conducting from a totally different score. In music this is called cacophony. In industry we rationalize it as "poor communication."

But engineering dissonance is more than a communication problem. It is systemic. It results from a failure to integrate diverse engineering functions into a unified process. It results from a failure to provide a unifying rationale for that process to follow. By fragmenting design, production, and quality engineering, we build barriers between functions that are interactive and interlocked. By failing to manage those functions as a customer-oriented value process, we promote insular and dogmatic engineering practice.

Technology and Value Perceptions

Customer perceptions of value change as technology changes. What satisfied travel requirements in the days of propeller-driven aircraft is totally unacceptable in the days of jet and supersonic transport. What was cost-effective when processing data employed punched cards and tabulating equipment is clearly cost-prohibitive today. So for engineering to be a value-creating process, it must adapt to technology change; it must employ technology to satisfy customer requirements more effectively.

The obstacles to achieving that objective are formidable; but two deserve comment. The first is that engineering is often locked into standards that easily deter adapting to change. Second, changes in technology are cumulative in their impact; but they do not occur at the same rate in all industries or in all engineering disciplines. Let's consider the matter of standards first.

In breaking down engineering into specialized tasks, we

establish and apply standards. We have design standards concerning performance and reliability characteristics of components, materials, dimensions, and tolerances employed in product design. These are manifest in drawings, formulas, bills of materials, and parts lists.

We have production standards for processes, methods, operations, and equipment. These include technical specifications, testing and inspection criteria and methods, machine setup drawings, and operation sheets.

We have purchasing standards covering specifications for materials, parts, equipment and services employed in design and production.

These standards simplify engineering tasks and are a basic feature of all engineering systems. Indeed, production and marketing could not easily take place without them. Nor could we produce products with common materials and components, or have interchangeability of parts to ensure continuing production and supply. Without standards we could not communicate internally or to outside suppliers about material, process, or performance requirements, and what it takes to satisfy them.

But engineering standards have a downside. They can be confining or restrictive. They can be out of date or not reflective of the latest developments. When imposed, they can stifle creativity and innovation. This is a particular problem where technology is expanding. As scientific discoveries produce new bodies of knowledge, engineering standards may become obsolete. This is precisely what Timken's Leibensperger was referring to when he described design engineers using computer tools to design products but incorporating material and property standards that were antiquated.[2]

This leads us to the second obstacle to engineering's adapting to technology change and employing it to satisfy customer-value perceptions. Technology is expanding but not uniformly in all industries or in all engineering disciplines. Customer requirements may call for the application of technologies from the mechanical, electronic, and chemical industries at one and the same time. They may involve the application of optical engineering, circuitry engineering, acoustical engineering, again at one and the same time. How does an engineering organization master each of these technologies? How does it incorporate them in products and processes when they are at different stages of discovery and development? To understand the enormity of this obstacle, consider the evolution of only two areas of technology.

Machinery, metalworking, and other industries built around mechanical engineering developed in the early 1900s. They grew up in an era of relatively slow scientific discovery, slow technological change. They developed in parallel with the mass-production automotive, appliance, and consumer-product industries. They were driven by the demands of those industries for consistent quality and lower costs. And to meet those demands, they promoted the development and application of engineering standards. The slower the rate of scientific discovery and technology change in those industries and their markets, the more those standards found reflection in subsequent design and production engineering.

In contrast, the electronics industry evolved in the latter half of the twentieth century. This was a period of significant scientific discovery. It was a period of rapid technological change. The industry was driven by the demands of both the military and commercial sector for enhanced product performance, improved reliability, and, very importantly, miniaturization. This demanded new concepts, new engineering approaches. Reliance on standards had to give way to reliance on innovation. And as technology fed upon itself, the industry spawned thousands of entrepreneurial specialists who were continuously defining and redefining standards.

What was happening in electronics was happening similarly in computers, telecommunications, biochemistry, and other newly emerging industries.

So What Do We Do?

To employ technologies successfully and to make engineering a true value-contributing process, we must change our notions of how to structure engineering tasks and how to manage them for value results.

To begin with, we must recognize that we cannot master all technologies. We should concentrate on those areas where we have engineering excellence and rely on outside sources to complement them. The not-invented-here syndrome is a particularly insidious and debilitating behavior pattern. It hides behind purported concerns for product performance or product quality. It raises fears about market acceptance and customer satisfaction. But the not-invented-here behavior pattern saps valuable engineering resources. And too often, it results in marginal, even inferior, design and production.

A company that has painfully learned this lesson is Digital Equipment. For five consecutive years it experienced steadily declining earnings. In the face of increasing competition from smaller and more nimble hardware and software suppliers, the company was losing market share, and even technical credibility. Historically, DEC has been a pure engineering-driven company. But technology was changing too fast and market demands were becoming too specialized for DEC engineering to keep pace. It was too oriented to developing products around its existing architecture, rather than meeting user needs with leading-edge hardware and software, regardless of their source.

In early 1993 Digital introduced a new program inviting VARs (value-added resellers) and ISVs (integrated-systems vendors)—important marketing channels for DEC—to take on a major role in product development and engineering support. In announcing the program, David Chen, DEC's area channels product marketing manager, made the following comments:

> We want to co-engineer products with VARs. . . . Instead of being viewed only as an extension of [DEC's] sales organization, VAR's and ISV's will be extensions of our engineering operations. [VARs and ISVs] are best suited to provide enabling technologies that will make our products more attractive to users. . . . In the proprietary world of the mid–70s and early 80s, we wanted to do everything. . . . Open systems have made those efforts redundant. . . . Instead of reinventing the

wheel, we're learning to work with VAR and ISV partners who are the original inventors.[3]

For a company that long prided itself on its engineering
prowess and its ability to define customer needs, to admit openly
its shortcomings is surprising. But the fact is that VARs add value
to DEC's engineering by providing problem-solving solutions to
closely targeted market segments. And ISVs add value by integrating DEC hardware and software into larger and more solu-
tion-specific systems and networks. In doing so, they become
vital components of the company's engineering process. They
become critical value contributors in satisfying customer performance and cost demands.

Outside Suppliers and the Engineering Process

It took five years of declining earnings to reverse Digital Equipment's not-invented-here engineering mode. It took catastrophic
losses in a much shorter period of time for that same mode to be
altered at IBM.

A dramatic example of that change is seen in IBM's introduction of its new laptop computer. Industry channels and trade
media have been glowing in their praise, and all agree it fills a
void in the company's product line. Dataquest Inc., a market
research firm in the industry, predicted that IBM would go from
no presence in the $6 billion world market to a 12 percent share
in the first year.[4]

Yet for three years, the company had tried and failed to
develop a technically acceptable and broadly marketable product.
The problem lay in the IBM product-development process. It took
too long; too many people were involved in the process. Detailed
specifications would be written for every part and component.
They would be reviewed, discussed, agreed to, or challenged. In
the event of challenge they would be written and reviewed again.
They would then move through a hierarchical maze for further
review and, ultimately, approval.

This engineering approach could work in markets that IBM
dominated or in markets where technology changed slowly. But

in the work station, PC, and laptop markets, technology was changing rapidly. According to press reports, IBM started development of the laptop already a generation behind on screen technology. It never caught up, and in 1989 withdrew from that market. And what it lacked in screen technology, it lacked in other technology areas as well.

In 1990 the company made a complete about-face. It formed development teams empowered to cut across traditional lines and to take calculated risks. Instead of incorporating previously employed IBM components in the laptop's design, engineering teams worked with outside suppliers to develop components specifically for the laptop. With the major exception of a few chips and the keyboard, outside sources engineered and supplied almost all of the parts assembled in the machine. Even the critical "mother" circuit board was designed and produced by Western Digital Corporation.

The DEC and IBM cases are clear illustrations of an engineering fact of life. No company can be a leader in all technologies. Scientific knowledge and discovery are expanding too fast to try keeping abreast, let alone leading in them all. The best strategy is to concentrate on core capabilities and rely on technology transfer from other sources to fill the void.

Marketing channels and suppliers are two critical technology sources. Marketing channels are the bridge to ultimate customers. Through market research and application engineering, they define customer problems and problem-solving solutions. Outside suppliers complement internal capabilities through advanced technology in specialized materials, components, and manufacturing methods. Both marketing channels and outside suppliers enhance the effectiveness of engineering. Both improve its meshing with other processes in the value network. This is how we adapt to technology change. This is how we employ it successfully in satisfying customer-value perceptions.

Who and What Is Engineering?
Restructuring the Engineering Process

We define *engineering* as the application of scientific knowledge to practical use. As such, the practice of engineering is generic to most business functions. It is generic by methodology. It is generic by discipline. Electrical engineering is electrical engineering whether it's employed in product design or in plant maintenance. Mechanical engineering is mechanical engineering whether we use it in laying out a manufacturing process or in purchasing close tolerance castings and forgings.

Yet, we ignore the generic nature and practice of engineering by organizing engineering within narrowly defined functional structures. We combine engineering disciplines involved in what we call product design and development in an engineering department. We combine those same engineering disciplines involved in producing the product in a manufacturing department.

Often, the determination of when design and development end and production begins is vague or poorly defined. Too often, it's arbitrary. In any event, by functionalizing engineering, we set up barriers between functions that are naturally linked by common engineering discipline. We build in redundancy and time lags between processes like engineering and manufacturing, which are interacting processes in a common value network.

A company that recognizes this redundancy and time lag and has done something different to address it is the Quantum Corporation. Its approach is to let design engineers do product design, and to let other tasks in the engineering process involving common engineering disciplines be performed where they can be performed more effectively.

One task specifically identified is that of material and component engineering, that is, specifying and developing requirements and sources for materials going into product designs. In most companies this function is typically performed in design or product engineering. At Quantum, it is performed jointly by design engineering and procurement.

Quantum is a major producer of 2.5-inch and 3.5-inch computer drives. Its customers are companies like Apple, Compaq, and Hewlett-Packard, and its market is highly dynamic and volatile. Life cycles on drives are steadily being compressed, and prices are declining at 3 to 8 percent, on average, per quarter. Given this scenario, the name of the game is "Get to market fast and right or get steamrollered by competition."

Quantum's forte is drive technology. Yet its products are manufactured with state-of-the-art ASICs (application-specific integrated circuits), drive heads and motors, and precision-made die castings, stampings, and machined parts. To expect design engineering to master these technologies as well as drive technology is unrealistic. To follow the conventional pattern of design engineering's defining product requirements and component engineering's specifying material requirements and then procurement's buying to purchase specifications is time-consuming. It also involves redundant effort in engineering and procurement.

Quantum's approach was to hire sixteen degreed engineers, with eight more to follow, who would serve as commodity engineers working closely with design engineering and suppliers. Their charter is to know all there is to know about the technologies the company buys. Commodity engineers help develop initial purchase specifications and propose modifications where specifications are unnecessary or costly. They do supplier selection and sourcing and have full responsibility for part or component performance. This includes the monitoring of supplier processes, quality control, and reliability.

Quantum's vice president of worldwide operations, John Pierre Patkay, says this about the commodity engineer approach:

> Most of us in the electronics industry have both a high materials content and a high technology content in the materials we purchase. . . . It's important to have a repository of knowledge, especially in a business with such a rapid time-to-market. The commodity engineer and manager teams make us a knowledgeable customer, which in turn improves our relations with suppliers.[5]

Patkay's comments are echoed by Quantum's suppliers. Bob Bailey, director of AT&T's ASIC product line says:

> [Quantum's] commodity engineers set the strategy for the program, and the time frame within which everything needs to be accomplished. They understand our

processes and can go line item by line item with us in the test program to determine what tests or specs aren't necessary. This helps us improve our quality, costs, and manufacturing, which nets us both savings.[6]

Quantum's linking of design engineering and component engineering is an approach employed also at Hewlett-Packard. Indeed, as a supplier to H-P, Quantum has undoubtedly been influenced by its customer's success in reducing development cycle times. Hewlett-Packard's approach, however, goes one step further. It not only links design engineering with what H-P calls materials engineering; it links both with manufacturing.

At Hewlett-Packard, this is performed through a process known as Systems and Product Introduction, nicknamed SPRINT. It is physically located within the engineering department and is jointly funded by engineering and manufacturing. Interestingly, however, it reports to materials management.

Each development project goes through four phases: investigation, design, prototyping, and pilot run. The task of SPRINT is to work with product designers and suppliers in all four phases to structure a bill of material that:

1. Accurately reflects product-design requirements
2. Is complete and sufficiently detailed for manufacturing planning and quality control

William Walker, materials manager at H-P Rockaway, New Jersey, describes how SPRINT works:

Every time a product is introduced, Manufacturing is given the opportunity to improve its competitiveness. For example, cycle times can be trimmed by carefully engineering the product's structure. . . . One of the keys to becoming more flexible and more competitive is the simplification of a new product's BOM [bill of materials]. A product with a design that specifies many subassemblies and a BOM with many levels has a long manufacturing cycle time. If the design can be simplified, then the product's BOM can be shortened. The result is a faster cycle time.[7]

At each stage of the four-phase development cycle, materials management plays an important engineering role. At the investigative stage it seeks out suppliers who can meet product engineering's technology needs. At the design stage it works with engineering and suppliers to develop component design and performance specifications. At the prototype and pilot-run stages, it ensures that last-minute changes are accurately incorporated in a final BOM. Manufacturing requires strict discipline in the formulation of a bill of materials, and once production begins, changes or corrections become costly.

Locating engineering tasks in nonengineering organizations, or performing them through cross-function teams, is a growing pattern in advanced-technology industry. It speeds up the engineering process by performing tasks concurrently, rather than sequentially. In both the Quantum and Hewlett-Packard examples, component engineering is performed simultaneously with design engineering. There is little or no time lag between product design and component specification, sourcing, and quality control. There is no redundancy of effort in design engineering and procurement. This makes for improved product performance, improved product reliability, and faster completion of the design-to-market cycle. It makes for closer integration of the engineering process with other processes in the value network.

Compressing Engineering Cycle Times

In today's dynamic and volatile markets, time is an increasingly important dimension of value perception. Markets are won or lost by the speed of new-product introduction. Customers remain customers only if their performance and cost requirements are met in a timely fashion. So, for engineering to be a true value-contributing process, it must satisfy not only the technical but also the time demands of the marketplace.

New-product development is an engineering subprocess involving five areas of activity:

1. *Conception.* Includes technical analysis and research leading to a new-product idea.
2. *Design engineering.* Includes preliminary design and design detailing.
3. *Testing and validation of final design against design criteria.*
4. *Process planning and process design.* Defines how the product will be produced.
5. *Prototype production.* Includes ramp-up to full production.

To speed up that process, we must compress these activities within shorter time spans. We do that either by reducing the time expended by individual activity, or by performing activities simultaneously rather than sequentially.

It is a truism that time is cost and cost impacts time, and new-product development is a process that clearly demonstrates that time-cost relationship. In a revealing study by *Computer-Aided Manufacturing*, it was found that although design is a small part of the development process, it locks in the greatest part of all subsequent spending. Hence, the more effectively we satisfy market and customer demands in initial design, the greater is the payback in cost and time later. Conception and design engineering account for a mere 5 to 8 percent of actual cost incurred, but they predetermine 60 to 80 percent of all subsequent cost.[8]

In a complementary study, Dataquest, a research firm in the computer and electronics industry, showed the effect on cost when design changes are made during the product-development process. These costs escalate from a mere $1,000 when changes are made in the design phase to a whopping $10 million during final production.[9]

These costs reflect time in a two-dimensional sense. Explicitly, they reflect quantitative time in terms of man-hours expressed as dollars and cents of cost. Implicitly, however, they reflect calendar time in terms of stretched-out schedules and completion dates. More man-hours expended invariably translates into longer time cycles from design to production. So changes made after design escalate not only cost but development time.

The conclusions we are forced to draw from these studies are clear:

1. We must address all engineering requirements at the time we conceptualize the product idea or begin design engineering. This includes identifying and defining:

- *Process requirements*—equipment, tooling, manufacturing methods; considerations of internal make versus external buy
- *Material and component requirements*—their design and performance characteristics, their sources of supply
- *Quality, reliability, and maintainability requirements*
- *Cost requirements*—both cost to the customer implicit in product design, and cost of manufacturing implicit in both product and process design

2. We must complete the engineering process before production begins. Once production begins, it's too late. Changes are costly and time-consuming.

This is the meaning of concurrent or simultaneous engineering. It's designing the product and the process that manufactures the product at the same time. It's integrating within a common time frame engineering tasks that are now fragmented and performed in some step-by-step sequence. As a means of speeding up the engineering process, the concept is gaining wide acceptance among companies competing on a rapid time-to-market strategy. But its success stories provide valuable lessons for all companies:

- Through concurrent engineering, Navistar, formerly International Harvester, developed a new truck for U-Haul International. The truck sits closer to the road and is easier to load. These are two important advantages over trucks U-Haul had been buying from Ford Motor Company. Within one year after design began, trucks were coming off the assembly line. This is against a minimum of three years, which it previously took for Harvester to custom-design and build trucks.

- By simultaneous engineering, Deere reduced its development time for construction and forestry equipment from seven years to a little more than four. In so doing it also reduced its cost of development by 30 percent.

- Ford reduced the cycle time of product development on the Taurus from its normal six years to two years. Ford applies concurrent engineering with its suppliers as critical participants in its development process. Allied Signal's Bendix Automotive Division is responsible for the entire brake system, from basic design to production supply. TRW begins design work on air bags and seat belts on the basis of a model's preliminary design. Fully 70 percent of all Ford's purchases are made from suppliers who concurrently engineer components.

In a survey performed for the Pentagon by the Institute for Defense Analysis, eleven companies were studied on how they applied concurrent engineering. The companies included General Electric, IBM, 3M, Hewlett-Packard, and Du Pont. They were analyzed in terms of the impact on time, cost, and profit by engineering for manufacturability, quality, and ease of maintenance at the time of initial product design. Development time was 30 to 70 percent less and time to market 20 to 90 percent less, while return on assets rose by 20 to 120 percent.[10]

These are impressive results and prove that concurrent engineering produces benefits well beyond its more highly publicized benefit of reducing development cycle times.

Compressing engineering tasks into shorter time spans—or concurrent engineering—has been promoted largely in new-product development. But the concept is equally applicable in processes that modify, adapt, or enhance existing product to unique customer specifications. Analysis of those processes identifies the following activities:

- Interpreting customer requirements and defining preliminary specifications

- Finalizing specifications and setting cost, price, and delivery requirements
- Preliminary design—combining new features with existing products; redesign or rearrangement of components from existing design
- Final design including specification and test documentation
- Release to manufacturing

These activities involve functions as diverse as sales, design engineering, manufacturing engineering, purchasing, and quality control. Typically, they follow some sequential routing through functional departments, one task beginning when a previous one ends. Each task involves multiple steps. Interpreting customer requirements and defining specifications, for example, is a two- to three-step exercise. Developing and finalizing design may take five or six steps. But these tasks need not be routed through separate functional departments. They need not be done sequentially. Getting sales manufacturing and quality control involved in preliminary design improves the total design process. Getting purchasing involved in component specification and sourcing improves it further.

It is entirely possible that this up-front involvement may lengthen the time to finalize design. But this is more than offset by the reduction in time resulting from fewer design changes and from the fact that final design will reflect a manufacturing process better able to produce a quality product, reliably and in shorter time.

Restructuring Engineering: Cross-Functional Teams

Whether it's speeding up the development cycle or improving product quality, companies have achieved their objective only when they restructured the engineering process. Restructuring takes many forms, varying from company to company, even from division to division in the same company. It is influenced by differences in products and processes, differences in the pace of technology change, differences in management philosophy and attitudes.

Restructuring might involve combining functions like production engineering and quality engineering with advanced design, product design and test in a single expanded engineering department. It might involve just the opposite tack, reducing the engineering department and moving functions like component engineering into procurement or production engineering into manufacturing. One large company formerly had a corporate R&D department that carried development through the prototype stage with tested models, manufacturing drawings, and parts lists ready to release to manufacturing. This process has been restructured by creating a plant-by-plant function known as product engineering, which handles:

- Final development of the product-production design, tooling, methods of fabrication, assembly testing
- Product improvement, even though this may involve the functions of the product or its components
- Tool design, production engineering, and process engineering

Only engineering research and advanced design remain in corporate R&D.

Each organizational approach, in its own way, aims at improving the overall process, and in some cases they may all succeed. But each suffers from a common problem. Once we place engineering functions in formal departmental structures, we institutionalize them. We give them a life of their own—a reason for being that often transcends broader technical and business objectives. So instead of improving the process, organizational restructuring often weakens it. This is particularly the case if we measure performance by narrow department and functional criteria.

It is for this reason that the most widely employed approach to restructuring engineering has been a less formalized approach. It has been through cross-functional teams. Every example I cited of shortening the development cycle time employed cross-functional teams. And the same is true for programs pursuing improved product quality or reduced product cost.

Cross-functional teams restructure the engineering process because they work outside the constraints of the formal organization. They are not locked into procedures, work-flow patterns, reporting and control systems that are features of the formal engineering structure. By cutting across functional lines, teams can circumvent or shortcut these roadblocks. By focusing on project goals, like reducing development cycle times, rather than on functional goals, teams construct an engineering process more market or customer oriented.

Of course, not all cross-functional teams are successful. Some are poorly led. Some are not staffed with knowledgeable and experienced team members. Some are provided with limited resources, or have limited stature and clout to command them. In too many instances, teams are unsuccessful because goals are not clearly defined or not strongly supported by higher management.

If any one company stands out for its successful employment of teams to improve the engineering process, it is Hewlett-Packard. This is a $16-billion-a-year producer of precision electronic products and systems that maintains an incredibly high rate of technical innovation. More than half its sales come from products developed within the past three years, and fully 60 percent of its R&D finds its way into product applications. Whether it's printers and PCs, medical instrumentation, or measurement systems, H-P fields cross-functional teams to speed up development time, improve performance and reliability, and facilitate technology transfer with customers, suppliers, and other processes.

Hewlett-Packard is deeply committed to innovation. And when it forms teams for that purpose it gives them wide authority to implement it. For example, on H-P's miniaturized Kitty Hawk disk drive, a cross-functional team pulled out all the stops to speed up product introduction. It spent $100,000 buying out a chip maker's entire production run. This allowed the supplier to concentrate only on H-P's prototypes, thereby reducing fabrication time by three weeks. Instead of designing and equipping a new production line to produce the drives in-house, the company farmed out the drives to Japan's Citizen Watch Company. Where normal development time would be minimally eighteen months, the Kitty Hawk drive took only a year.

One of the strong reasons why Hewlett-Packard's teams have been so successful is that they operate in an organizational environment that is more functionally integrated than most. In the mid 1980s, the company reorganized engineering to eliminate the sharp divisions between design engineering and manufacturing engineering. Its goal was to interlock the two functions so that they would literally lose their separate identity. According to an *Industry Week* article on world-class organizations, H-P's rule of thumb was: "If you can walk into a company and distinguish between engineering and manufacturing, something is wrong."

Boon Hwee-Koh, managing director of Hewlett-Packard-Singapore, describes the company's philosophy in the following terms: "The goal must be to destroy the barriers separating design engineers, production engineers, and manufacturing engineers. Functional goals need to be sacrificed for shared objectives." Koh emphasizes that engineering should be integrated. "The thinking has to span the distance from how suppliers make the parts to how they're assembled to the customer's expectation of quality."[11]

Given so enlightened a view of the engineering process, it is not surprising that Hewlett-Packard enjoys great success with cross-functional teams. Also given its management aspirations, company success should continue and flourish.

John Young, H-P's CEO, is dedicated to reducing what he calls "break-even time," that is, the period from the introduction of a technology to its profitable implementation. It now takes the company eighteen to twenty-four months to recover its costs of new-product development. Young expects to cut that time in half by the year 2000. This is a powerful challenge, demanding the closest teamwork not only within the engineering process but among all processes in the H-P value network.

Engineering and Internal Customers in the Value Network

Engineering creates and contributes value by designing and developing products and applications that satisfy customer requirements at least total cost of acquisition, ownership, and use.

Necessarily, least cost of acquisition, ownership, and use includes the price at which the customer buys. Hence, competitive price is a factor in the purchaser's perception of value. But total cost includes the cost of installing, operating, or consuming what is bought. It includes the cost of handling, storing, maintaining, and repairing what is bought. It includes the cost of not receiving what is bought. This includes the cost of performance or quality failure, the cost of inadequate service and product support, and the cost of late delivery or completion dates.

Although many involved in the engineering process are aware of these costs, they often fail to reflect that awareness in their actions. They are diverted by more-immediate concerns like designing for a price-competitive advantage or developing a product application to meet some arbitrary deadline. More often than not, those concerns stem from higher-management pressure to achieve some limited or short-term objective. They stem from management's viewing engineering as a cost- and time-consuming process rather than a value-creating one.

Some in engineering may also fail to recognize customer costs when they see product design and development as an end in itself, rather than a means to customer satisfaction. Thus, designing for product performance or reliability can easily become designing for maximum performance, maximum reliability. This means incorporating the best, the surest, the safest features and elements in the product's design. It also means stretched-out development and testing time, not to mention compromises—often costly ones—on other design features. Ease of operation and ease of maintenance are two commonly compromised features. Manufacturability and ease of sourcing are two others.

The point is that engineering has other customers. These are internal ones. They are the marketing, acquisition, manufacturing, and customer service processes that make up the company's value network. Their "requirements" are for products and information that engineering supplies.

They include marketing and customer service requirements for product and performance specifications, operating manuals, installation, maintenance, and repair instructions. They include acquisition and manufacturing requirements for drawings and purchase specifications, bills of materials, testing and inspection criteria and methods, operation flow sheets, equipment setup drawings. And like external customers, internal customers receive value when these requirements are satisfied at least cost in use.

It is part of the current management jargon to espouse being "customer oriented." But it is truly surprising how few companies recognize customers as being internal as well as external. Yet it is the internal customers who ultimately satisfy the external ones. It is those value-creating, value-adding processes that supply value as external customers acknowledge it. And the criteria of value are the same for both—satisfaction of requirements at least total cost.

For engineering to be a true value contributor in a value network, it must recognize these internal customers and satisfy their requirements cost-effectively.

Chapter 5

Value and the Acquisition Process

It has always been a puzzle to me how managements have failed to acknowledge acquisition as a value-contributing process. In many respects this is a consequence of the mass-production reasoning that continues to surface in much of our business theory and practice. The nub of that reasoning is that:

- Marketing and sales identify and influence customer perceptions of value.
- Engineering specifies and designs to satisfy value requirements.
- Manufacturing produces and supplies value as marketing and engineering define it.

Under this reasoning, procurement and logistics are merely service functions of manufacturing and marketing. They don't compose a value-contributing process in their own right.

This line of reasoning was probably true in the early days of mass production. It was clearly true in the early days of automobile manufacturing. The Model T Ford, for example, was introduced in 1908 and reached peak production in the early 1920s. Throughout that period its design remained the same. It was produced by a process that changed only from a series of stationary workplaces to a moving assembly line. The Model T was assembled from standard and interchangeable components, largely produced by Ford itself, or by captive suppliers. Under those circumstances the acquisition process—if we can even use that term—was a routine, clerical task. It involved scheduling requirements and placing orders for materials and parts and then routing them from source of supply to some stores or staging site.

But that's not the nature of the automotive industry today. Nor is it the nature of the electronics, telecommunications, computer or any other industry experiencing growth and expanding technology. It's not even the nature of more stable and mature industries like steel, chemicals, and paper products. The industry pattern today, and for the foreseeable future, is for companies to be lean and flexible, to concentrate on high-value-added core capabilities, and to outsource as much as they can. Outsourcing may be through purchase, subcontract, leasing, licensing, partnering, or strategic alliances. But essentially it is acquiring values from outside suppliers to complement those created and produced internally. And this is achieved through the process I call acquisition.

Acquisition involves the specifying of purchased materials, components, and services going into products and systems. On complex systems, specifications can cover thousands, even tens of thousands, of discrete line items. Many of these must be designed and built to meet unique performance or application requirements. To produce them demands special tooling and in some instances even special facilities and manufacturing equipment. These too must be specified.

The acquisition process includes the planning and scheduling of quantities and due dates. It includes the setting and implementing of quality standards that each material and component must meet. The process develops sources, invites and evaluates proposals, and negotiates agreements with suppliers and contractors. It contracts for and administers physical transportation, inbound from suppliers and outbound to customers and points of distribution. The process inspects, handles, and stores what is received and moves it to its point of use.

All of this is an integrated process of planning, purchasing, traffic, and stores functions. It is a process that interacts with other functions and processes like design engineering and quality control, manufacturing and marketing. It is a value-contributing process that provides time-and-place utility to supplier products and services within the value network, time-and-place utility to finished products to outside customers and markets.

Looking at the Numbers

To understand the importance of this process in today's industrial scene, let's consider only one of its functions—purchasing. However, let's do so by looking at it within the context of company sales and product costs. This will put it into a larger and more meaningful perspective.

According to a *Purchasing* magazine survey, purchases of the top one hundred companies in 1992 represented on average 42 percent of sales and 60 percent of product cost.[1] Expressing it another way, 42 cents out of every sales dollar and 60 cents out of every dollar of product cost went out on purchased materials and supplies.

For some companies the percentages were considerably higher—67 percent of sales and 70 percent of product cost at Chrysler; 56 percent of sales and 69 percent of product cost at Navistar; 41 percent of sales and 90 percent of product cost at Apple Computer. And this did not even include purchases of construction, capital equipment, maintenance, repair, and professional services. It did not include the outsourcing of data processing, engineering, and clerical labor. It did not include expenditures for licenses, leases, or rentals. Even excluding these other expenditures, purchased materials and supplies were five to six times the cost of manufacturing labor. Yet we still think of purchasing as a service and support to manufacturing.

For years we have looked at the Japanese manufacturing system as a model for our own; so the Japanese experience may well be an indicator of what's likely to come. According to a study by Tokyo Metropolitan University in 1990, Japanese labor costs were a mere 5 percent of total manufacturing costs. Capital equipment and administration made up 25 percent of costs, while material and subcontracting accounted for 70 percent.[2]

As we automate and downsize further, labor will continue to shrink as a percentage of manufacturing cost, while purchase expenditures for materials, subcontracting, and outsourcing will grow. They will grow in all industries, but they'll grow fastest where technology is expanding and where competition is volatile or global. Management will be forced to recognize that the safest and least costly way of acquiring advanced technology and reducing market risks is through outside sourcing.

Acquisition Myopia

Theodore Levitt wrote about "marketing myopia." With all due respect, I would like to borrow his phrasing to describe another aberration in management perception, what I call acquisition myopia. It is the failure to see acquisition as a value-adding process. It is a failure to recognize that the process is more than routine clerical tasks. It is the integration of subprocesses and functions that must be managed effectively for value results.

The primary subprocesses of acquisition are procurement and logistics. By *procurement* I mean all purchasing, subcontracting, outsourcing, leasing, partnering from and with suppliers. By *logistics* I mean the physical handling, storing, and moving of materials and products from source of supply to point of use or distribution.

Management is the planning, scheduling, implementing, and measuring of functions and resources to achieve defined objectives. Acquisition objectives are:

1. To satisfy the requirements of internal customers for materials, supplies, equipment, and services at least cost in use
2. To mesh with other processes within the value network in creating and supplying values as external customers acknowledge and perceive them

This is a process distinct from manufacturing. It is also a process demanding the employment of management and functional disciplines. These realities are easily overlooked, because acquisition activities are manufacturing related and they are repetitive.

We requisition, purchase, transport, and store materials and repeat these steps for each discrete manufacturing requirement. At each step in the procurement-manufacturing cycle, we create, store, and transmit information. In view of these activities management sees acquisition as merely a series of paper processing tasks, integrated solely through manufacturing data systems and simplified paperwork flow.

There is no question that procurement and logistics generate the greatest volume of data and paperwork within the business organization. That data and paperwork cover specifications and specification changes, requisitions, purchase orders, shipping instructions, bills of lading, receiving and inspection reports, inventory records, stores and disbursement records, work orders, scrap reports, invoices, etc. And the data are captured and processed for each material item and for each transaction. Clearly, that paperwork flow makes it a prime candidate for computerization, and computerizing it stigmatizes the activities that generate that flow as clerical tasks. Thus, computerized materials requirements planning (MRP) systems are invariably justified in terms of speedier data flow and reduced clerical and administrative manpower.

There is no question that MRP systems have vastly speeded up procurement and logistics paperwork flow. They have also provided important additional benefits. They have improved inventory levels and turnover rates, cut down lost production time due to material shortages, reduced both the direct and indirect costs of purchasing and manufacturing. Through their ability to project requirements, MRP systems have improved the caliber of planning and scheduling that results in better utilization of capacity and resources.

But MRP systems pose problems in today's technical and economic environment. To begin with, they were designed as manufacturing planning systems. They included procurement modules only because procurement activities initiate the paper-work flow to and through manufacturing. However, they dealt with only a small part of the procurement process. MRP was not designed to handle subcontracting, capital equipment and tool purchases, and outsourcing of manufacturing, engineering, and technical services. And with these becoming an increasingly larger share of product costs, MRP's logic and thrust is now poorly directed.

Second, MRP systems were designed around a continuous-flow manufacturing model. That is why they work best for production of uniform products, assembled from common and standardized components and produced at predictable rates and quality levels.

But with markets becoming more segmented and products becoming more customized, manufacturing is not continuous. It is small-batch production, using flexible manufacturing systems, to meet changing customer demands rapidly. It is simultaneous development and production of an ever changing product mix in ever shortening time cycles. It is manufacturing in a just-in-time (JIT) mode. And MRP systems were designed long before JIT was recognized as a manufacturing and inventory control discipline.

But to me the most serious problem MRP systems create is that they tend to become management systems rather than infor-mation systems: systems that make decisions rather than systems for planning. They generate data in so regimented a format that what was originally conceived as system "recommendations" become system directives. To illustrate:

■ MRP projections of materials may be 1,000 units, but sup-plier price discounts kick in at 1,200 units. Instead of analyzing the pros and cons of the larger purchase, we buy 1,000 units because that's what the "requirement" calls for.

■ Two part numbers are machined on the same lathe. MRP requirements call for 100 of part A and 50 of part B in week 1; 75 of part A and 100 of part B in week 2. Rather than analyzing the economics of combining quantities in a single setup run as against double setups for each part number, we machine the parts as the "requirements" dictate.

■ At one company I saw MRP generate requirements for identical electronic devices going into multiple assemblies under different customer order releases. Accordingly, 5 units of a device were the "requirement" for assembly A, order release 1; 3 units for assembly B, order release 2; and 8 units for assembly C, order release 3. Those were the "requirements" and that's the way they were requisitioned and purchased. Actually, that's the way the company did most of its purchasing.

I was retained to analyze the company's procurement system, and to make recommendations on how it might be improved. Looking at only three categories of purchased items—resistors, capacitors, and relays—and using a most conservative figure of $75 as the cost of placing a purchase order, I found that over a twelve-month period the company was incurring $186,000 of purchase order costs to acquire less than $10,000 of purchased materials.

The point is that functional decision-making is being abdicated, and the MRP system is doing the deciding. It's doing the deciding because:

1. The system generates so much data in such frequency that planners and buyers have trouble sorting, analyzing, and prioritizing it—all necessary steps before making intelligent acquisition decisions.
2. It's easier and even safer to let the system decide. Challenging "requirements" means possible confrontation between purchasing and planning, master scheduling and shop scheduling. This could entail personal risks that will outweigh any personal advantage.
3. The system has become untouchable because it cost a small fortune to design and implement and higher management approved the expenditure.

This is why the MRP problems I've cited receive little or no attention. Having paid the price to implement MRP, management is loath to recognize its shortcomings. It's particularly loath to recognize that the system was designed as a planning tool for a different business environment than what we know today. It is true that MRP has simplified and improved the planning and scheduling activities that support manufacturing. But planning and scheduling also support procurement and logistics. And procurement and logistics can contribute as much, if not more, to customer value as manufacturing.

But to acknowledge that is to acknowledge acquisition as a value-adding process distinct from manufacturing. And management may not be ready to make that acknowledgement. MRP systems provide a comforting illusion for viewing acquisition and manufacturing in traditional terms. But like all illusions they distort our view of reality.

Three Bids: Pick the Low Bidder

Another manifestation of the problem I call acquisition myopia can be seen in management notions about the nature of the procurement process and how it works. Consciously or unconsciously, those notions reflect the strong and continuing influence of government procurement philosophy over industrial procurement practice. This began with industrial mobilization during World War II and prevails even today.

As part of the war effort, industry converted plants and facilities from civilian to military production. It built new plants to turn out everything from canteens to canisters, from cannon to carrier aircraft. This meant new construction, new equipment and tooling, new sources of supply. And this demanded a procurement function capable of doing more than the clerical task of placing purchase orders and routing them through delivery. Fully 90 to 95 cents of every dollar appropriated for weapons and supplies was being spent by contractors to the military. So how contractors bought determined not only the quantity of weapons the military received, but also how quickly it received them.

As a result of these concerns, the military brought pressure on its contractors to improve the caliber of their procurement effort. Talent was recruited from engineering, manufacturing, and other functions to provide technical and logistical expertise.

Procurement was expanded to include additional functions like stores and traffic. In many cases it was reorganized to report directly to senior management. Meanwhile, government auditors monitored these developments for compliance with government instructions and procedures.

When we realize the scope and extent of industrial mobilization during the war, we can begin to understand the influence the military exerted over industry's procurement practices. That influence persists right up to the present day over all companies engaged in government business. These companies are audited regularly on their procurement process. The process is approved or disapproved on the basis of how it conforms to government policies and regulations. Disapproval is particularly onerous because it restricts the freedom of action not only of procurement but of all other activities as well. Disapproval means time-consuming review and prior approval by government contracting officers before purchases or subcontracts can be placed.

What are the essential features of government procurement policy? Implicit in the laws and regulations are three tenets:

1. Because public monies are expended, government procurement must avoid all favoritism, collusion, and fraud.

2. Because ours is a democratic society, whenever government agencies have purchase requirements, they must provide the widest opportunity for interested suppliers to supply.

3. Because ours is a market, competitive economy, the workings of the competitive process can satisfy government requirements at the "lowest responsible and responsive" bid price. By *responsible*, the law means that bidders are qualified to bid. By *responsive*, it means that bidders bid in accordance with the terms of the invitation and take no exception to them.

The consequence of these tenets is that the preferred method of government procurement is "full and open competition." Up until a few years ago it was formal, advertised bidding. The advertising of government requirements is no longer a condition of government procurement, but its formality is. The government specifies how bids will be prepared, when they will be submitted, how they will be evaluated, how a contract will be structured and awarded. In many cases, bids are sealed, and remain sealed until a public opening. Negotiation, involving discussions, analysis, and trade-offs on bid contents, is discouraged. It is employed only in the exception and is rigidly proscribed as to methods and practices allowed.

Whether companies employ sealed bid procedures or not, it is surprising how many managements believe that competitive bidding is the most effective way to buy. Consequently, all that's necessary to satisfy purchase requirements is to develop competition and buy from the lowest bidder. Since managements believe this is a relatively simple and straightforward process, it does not require exceptional talent or resources to implement.

Thus, procurement positions receive low job classifications and job ratings. They are generally compensated at a lower wage scale than comparable-level positions in engineering, manufacturing, or marketing. And purchasers are measured largely on price performance because lower prices are what management believes is purchasing's principal objective. Look at the assignment given to General Motors' former purchasing czar, J. Ignaco López de Arriortua. And look at GM's frantic efforts to keep its price-cutter par excellence from breaking ranks and moving to Volkswagen.

As a commentary on management's perception of the procurement function, compare the technical and financial support it receives as against the support manufacturing receives.

Staffing every manufacturing organization are manufacturing engineers, industrial engineers, quality engineers, cost estimators and cost controllers. Management recognizes that production, quality, and cost objectives could not be achieved unless this kind of knowledge and expertise were applied to the task. Yet it is a rarity to find a purchasing organization with the same experience and talent. It is assumed that competition will achieve the desired results, so that no technical, financial, or management effort is needed to make them happen. It is assumed that if suppliers are qualified—whatever that may mean—competition will satisfy quality, time, and service requirements at the lowest bid price.

This might be true if purchase requirements were for standard, off-the-shelf commodity items, readily available from sources of supply equally capable of satisfying them. But this is becoming more the exception than the rule.

■ Purchase requirements are for parts and components made to unique performance, application, and reliability specifications. Often they involve supplier design and development before they can be produced. This demands technical knowledge of products and processes.

■ Purchase requirements are for subcontracted assemblies or outsourced products, which formerly were manufactured in-house. Typically, they are single-sourced and they employ special tooling, equipment, process controls, and test and inspection procedures. This demands management's skill in planning and coordinating resources.

■ Purchase requirements are for quantities and delivery schedules closely tied into marketing and manufacturing programs. This demands monitoring the supplier production and inventory plans, capacity utilization, machine and manpower loading, and supplier performance against plan.

■ Purchase requirements are for product applications, engineering and technical services for which there is no "market" in the sense of an existing supply and measurable demand. They are produced and supplied to order, and prices are cost based rather than market driven. This calls for an understanding of cost and financial factors that determine price. They call for analytical skills to negotiate them effectively.

■ Purchase requirements are value requirements. And the lowest competitive price is not necessarily value. Value, or lowest cost of acquisition, ownership, and use, is only ascertainable after purchase requirements have been met. So the task of procurement is to manage for that result, to ensure that value purchased is in fact supplied.

The Conversion of AT&T

A company that learned that low-bid buying alone does not generate value results is AT&T. It learned that fact when the nature of its business changed. That change began in 1984 with the court-ordered breakup of the Bell System. It gained momentum with AT&T's expansion into equipment and component manufacturing markets. It accelerated further with the acquisition of NCR, formerly the National Cash Register Company.

With the breakup of Bell, AT&T lost the operating base of its intrastate telephone business, a base now serviced by the "Baby Bell" telephone companies. In losing that base it lost not only a captive consumer market—local telephone users—but also a captive market for the equipment, products, and services it supplied its subsidiaries through Bell Labs and Western Electric. The Baby Bells were now free to source their requirements wherever they saw fit.

Although AT&T retained its interstate and international business, it was now exposed to growing competition from companies like MCI, Sprint, and Advanced Telecommunications. And for the first time it was exposed to competition from its newly independent "offspring," who were now entering into strategic alliances with foreign telecommunication companies to jointly develop offshore markets.

With the acquisition of NCR, AT&T became more deeply involved with the cyclical and significantly more competitive world of computer and electronic products and systems. Not only was it taking on the established IBMs, DECs, and Intels; it was also going toe-to-toe with dozens of aggressive and innovative newcomers in integrated circuits, disk drives, and fax modems. And clearly, how AT&T did business before was ill suited to how it had to do business now.

As the owner and operator of the Bell System, AT&T was in a regulated industry. It was—and still is—subject to regulation by the FCC in its interstate business; it was subject to regulation by state public service or public utility commissions in each state within which it operated.

Supplying value in a regulated industry is vastly different from supplying it in a market driven by competition and changing customer demands. In a regulated industry, customer requirements are for reliable service priced at fair and reasonable rates. In the telephone business the ICC and public utility commissions are the monitor of what constitutes reliable service. They are also the arbiter of what are "fair and reasonable" rates. Necessarily, their assessments of both reflect public opinion expressed either through legislative bodies or through the media.

In AT&T's new business environment, customers are not some abstract market identifiable only by area code and telephone number. They're telecommunication systems providers, data systems integrators, computer and multimedia equipment manufacturers. Each customer has unique product design and performance requirements; each has critical time schedules for new-product development and introduction. Each customer is also subject to its own market and competitive pressures, making it acutely sensitive about internal costs and competitive prices.

In a regulatory environment, company purchases tend to follow government procurement practice. This is not difficult to understand when we realize that public utility commissions set rates on the basis of some return-on-investment formula. So any acquisition of physical plant and equipment, any increase in the materials and supply inventory could impact the rate-setting decision. And one criterion commissions employ to determine if a rate is fair and reasonable is whether purchases were competitively bid.

At AT&T this was the way the company bought. It developed multiple sources. It formally invited competitive bids to meet some specified closing date. It evaluated bids in bid-evaluation committees and awarded business on the basis of the bid responses. At every step in the procurement process, from specification through physical disbursement, there was detailed documentation to justify source selection and pricing.

Today, things are different. At AT&T's switchboard division the company produces transmission equipment, light-wave systems, digital radio systems, and digital terminals. Its purchasing and transportation managers who worked in both the regulated and nonregulated environment look back with few regrets on how the company bought before.

"In the old days if you didn't have two suppliers for everything, you weren't doing your job," says Ray Strauss, purchasing manager in charge of wiring boards, computer equipment, and fabricated parts. "The purchasing philosophy today is that you have to reduce your supply base and really get involved with one supplier. You just can't afford to have a supply base of ten suppliers for one part."[3]

In the old days AT&T also competitively rebid its business every three months. As Strauss describes it: "Then we'd go out to quote it again. Another supplier would quote a few cents less, so you went to that guy. The business would flip-flop back and forth. Now there are very few contracts that are less than three years."[4] And although the division has 600 production suppliers, 95 percent of its purchase dollars are spent with 240 "preferred suppliers." The very thought of preferred suppliers would have been anathema under the old AT&T approach.

All of this represents a radical change in AT&T buying practice from what prevailed before. And the results are impressive.

- By employing cross-functional buying teams from initial design through product introduction, the division has reduced its total cost of product by $400 million over a three-year period.
- With concentration of business with preferred suppliers, on-time delivery of purchased components is now 85 percent as against 50 percent in 1987.
- With establishment of long-term agreements and avoidance of competitive price shopping, supplier quality improvement, measured in parts per million, is twice that of the industry average.

As testimony that AT&T's process is now a value-contributing process, the switchboard division won the prestigious Malcolm Baldrige National Quality Award in 1992. This was public recognition that the division had achieved quality excellence in the markets it served. The division also received certification to ISO 9000, the international body of quality standards. It should be noted that an essential requirement to receive certification is an effective procurement process. It's clear that an AT&T employing its old methods of procurement could never have been certified.

The General Electric Story

For nearly thirty years I conducted purchasing training programs for the General Electric Company. My seminars and workshops dealt with topics like "Price and Cost Analysis" and "Contract Negotiation and Administration," but the program I presented most frequently was one called "Analytical Purchasing." This developed the concept of value buying, that is, buying to satisfy purchase requirements at least cost of acquisition, ownership, and use. Necessarily to do value buying, purchasers had to analyze supplier offerings in cost and value terms. They also had to negotiate and administer purchase agreements for value results.

During the years I consulted with GE, the company went through a number of organizational changes. Many of those changes affected how it performed its purchasing and related activities. For example, in the late 1950s and early 1960s, GE introduced what it called materials management. Under that concept, it integrated purchasing with production planning and control, traffic, and value analysis to create a single materials function.

Production planning and control included activities like master scheduling, materials and manufacturing planning, and inventory control. Traffic was essentially inbound transportation. Value analysis, as I described it in Chapter 1, was the formalized analysis of materials and components in terms of function and cost of function. Thus, *materials management* described the multifunction process of planning, scheduling, purchasing, and moving materials from their source of supply to their point of use. At the corporate level this was an administrative and oversight activity, but at the plant level it became the basic model for the procurement process.

From the mid-1970s on, General Electric went through more-extensive restructuring. As one of the world's largest—and certainly most diversified—companies, it was becoming unwieldy and not sufficiently responsive to market and technology changes. Accordingly, the company combined and consolidated businesses into strategic market groups and sectors. Multiproduct operations were broken down into strategic business units, and decentralization occurred on a mammoth scale. What was corporate materials management disappeared from the scene. Corporate purchasing remained but was severely cut back in size. Each group, division, department or plant organized its acquisition process to suit its own business needs. In most cases, the materials management model was kept in place; but the development of computerized manufacturing and materials requirements planning (MRP-I and II) drastically altered the mix and scope of activities it now performed.

Looking back over the years I have come to believe that General Electric is one of the most innovative companies in tailoring its acquisition process to the needs of the times. To begin with it was GE that pioneered the idea of value as least cost in use; and this was in the 1950s, a period of postwar scarcity and shortages. Through its promotion of value analysis and value engineering, it subjected manufacturing, material, and service requirements to the test of meeting the least cost criterion. This provided a powerful and consistent direction to procurement and logistics for satisfying requirements.

Again, it was General Electric that introduced the materials management approach. This was in the 1960s, a period of rapid economic growth. Materials management was a radical break with traditional ways of organizing functions like purchasing and production control. In most companies these were performed in separate departments, often reporting to different levels of management. This slowed up manufacturing, or worse resulted in production that was out of phase with marketing needs.

When these functions were combined within one department, reporting to the same management, a common source of friction was reduced. Purchasing could no longer pursue its own special interests, like buying from a lower-priced source, if that could jeopardize production schedules. Similarly, production control was constrained from pursuing such objectives as avoiding or reducing inventory, if that would handicap purchasing.

Both were integral functions in a common process of supplying materials to manufacturing in the right quantity and at the right time. And this was imperative if GE was to grow at a rate faster than the economy was growing.

In the 1970s and early 1980s, the combination of hyperinflation and stagnant growth posed new challenges to industry. General Electric was a leader in meeting that challenge through marketing and manufacturing decentralization. It also was a leader in structuring its procurement process to support that change. By breaking up its operations into strategic market units, the company rationalized its diverse business mix and provided a clearer focus for procurement. By integrating planning, scheduling, purchasing and traffic within a single product-oriented structure, it narrowed that focus even further. Functional differences that previously existed between purchasing and planning and purchasing and engineering gave way to interfunctional cooperation. Long before cross-function teams were even heard of, GE was employing them in a discipline known as business-managed procurement. This was employed at the division or plant level. It was employed on high-dollar-value, critical-use materials and components, and its aim was to satisfy manufacturing requirements at lower cost in use.

As a value-contributing process to its internal customer, manufacturing, GE's approach to acquisition received high marks, and that is not surprising. General Electric was a strongly manufacturing-oriented company, and activities like purchasing, production planning, and inventory control were always seen as service and support functions to manufacturing. By combining them through materials management, GE integrated those functions into a more effective acquisition process. But the thrust of that process was, first and foremost, to support manufacturing.

Therein lay the primary weakness in the GE approach. Its acquisition process was not focused on the needs of the ultimate customer, the marketplace. It was focused on manufacturing. Organizationally, it was not in the loop that directly identified and specified customer requirements and the means to satisfy them. To mesh with marketing and engineering, acquisition had to funnel through manufacturing. This could only bias its notions of value toward that perceived by manufacturing rather than that perceived by the ultimate customer. It also meant that the acquisition process would be slow and less effective in sourcing and implementing technology change from outside suppliers.

We now come full circle in the evolution of that process. In the past few years General Electric has gone through further restructuring. It has done so to deal more effectively with the challenges of the 1990s: global competition, rapidly expanding technology, and the growth of segmented and specialized markets. It has become a company that is both centralized and decentralized, and its acquisition process has followed suit.

Plants and departments are now combined into centrally managed business groups like appliances, lighting, motors, medical systems, power systems, and transportation. In each business group there is a centralized purchasing activity. There is also a centralized design engineering activity. This is a clear recognition that purchasing is a contributing function in the engineering process, while design engineering is a contributing function in the acquisition process. And these processes create and add value when they are meshed within a network by a common business and marketing strategy. They also work more effectively when physically they are located at a common site.

Group procurement buys materials and components that are unique to the product and service requirements of each business group. Corporate procurement, now called corporate business development, negotiates purchase agreements for materials and services that are common to all business groups—steel, copper, aluminum, electronic components, plastics, office supplies, and transportation services.

Thus, the company achieves maximum leverage on commodities and services with corporate volume. It promotes close cross-functional integration on materials and components with special design and application demands. And to ensure direct access to other processes in the value network, procurement reports directly to the business group president or one level immediately below.

It is interesting to trace the evolution of the acquisition process at General Electric. It went from:

- A centralized to a highly decentralized structuring of activities and functions, ultimately arriving at a synthesis of the two approaches
- A process seen largely as a service or support to manufacturing to another value-contributing process in a larger value network
- A process heavily influenced by functional concerns—buying at the right price, scheduling production for optimal machine and manpower loading—to one geared to customer satisfaction

As John Cologna, GE's corporate manager of business development expressed it to me, "We have removed functional barriers in procurement and logistics. We now recognize them only as an integrated process. And no function owns the process. Functions only have stakes in the process."

More Value-Adding Acquisition

Different companies pursue different value objectives through acquisition. Some seek quicker time to market. Others seek product-cost improvement. Still others seek a more effective means of implementing a marketing or business strategy. But regardless of the objective, whenever companies employ acquisition as a value-contributing process, the results can be dramatic.

CHRYSLER developed its new class of automobiles under a platform concept known as "cab-forward." This was a radically different approach to car design. Its aim was to provide more passenger room by moving the rear wheels farther back and extending the windshield farther forward. To do this posed problems like designing a smaller engine compartment and mounting the engine front-to-back, rather than side-to-side. It also called for an oversize windshield curving in two planes.

A key element in Chrysler's planning was to involve suppliers from the very beginning of the design process. According to Mike Ciccone, purchasing executive assigned to the program, this was never done before. Typically, purchasing did not line up suppliers until about 70 to 80 weeks before production. On this program, sourcing began 180 weeks before. Instead of the 600 to 700 suppliers usually employed in developing and producing a new model car, Chrysler now recruited only 200.

"Nothing was put out for bid," says Ciccone.[5] Suppliers were selected on the basis of technical and production capability. Every detail of Chrysler engineering, production, and market planning was shared with suppliers. This enabled them to make the necessary investments in equipment and personnel. In every sense, suppliers selected on the program became extensions of Chrysler. They were even given their own key to the company's technology center in Auburn Hills, Michigan.

Integrating suppliers within Chrysler's design and development employed acquisition as a value-contributing process. And the payoff to the company has been substantial. Its cab-forward, or LH, cars, as they are also known, were developed in thirty-nine months, almost half the time it previously took. This enabled Chrysler to hit the market sooner with more innovative and customer-friendly models. The cars were also developed and introduced at costs well under budget. This enabled the company to remain price competitive.

BRIGGS & STRATTON is the world's largest producer of cooled gasoline engines ranging in size from two to eighteen horsepower. It is a large purchaser of aluminum, which is a basic material from which the engines are made. Through value-adding acquisition, the company has achieved the next best thing to having an aluminum producer build a smelter on or near its Milwaukee facility. Every two hours of each working day, supplier trucks arrive from as far away as 300 miles delivering molten aluminum to the small engine manufacturer's plant. Each truck carries 35,000 pounds of molten aluminum, which is poured into one or two holding tanks. Each truck driver also brings a sample disk and a computer printout that details the molten aluminum's chemical composition. This confirms that the shipment delivered meets all specification requirements.

Briggs & Stratton builds five to five and a half million small air-cooled four-cycle aluminum engines a year, and aluminum represents approximately one third of the company's total dollar purchases. With that volume it enjoys obvious price advantage. But by integrating raw materials supply and logistics within a value-adding acquisition process, it enjoys more substantial and long-lasting benefits. It has increased the number of inventory turns, thereby reducing the cost of capital tied up in inventory. It has sharply reduced lead times, thereby reducing the cost of manufacturing losses due to material shortage or stockout. It has improved manufacturing yields by ensuring that molten aluminum delivered to the point of use meets all specification requirements.

MICHAELS STORES OF DALLAS is a $500 million arts and crafts retail chain with 144 stores from coast to coast. It purchases roughly half of what it sells offshore, largely from Pacific Rim suppliers. In the 1980s, Michaels bought direct from those suppliers. Its internal buying operation would develop sources, negotiate prices, and arrange transportation from the Far East to U.S. storage and distribution points.

In 1990 Michaels changed its acquisition strategy. Instead of buying direct and arranging its own transportation, Michaels decided to buy from U.S.-based importers. The reasoning was that this would streamline the acquisition-marketing process. It would avoid the problems of dealing with offshore sources, monitoring transocean carriers, and dealing with insurance and customs. The strategy made sense, but it was expensive. Michaels found that it was paying as much as 25 percent more for bulk items than it had paid when it bought direct. With that kind of cost disadvantage, it could not compete effectively.

In 1992, on the basis of its previous experience, Michaels decided to go back to direct importing. However, it decided also to do it differently. Its buyers would still develop sources and negotiate deals with offshore vendors, but Michaels would outsource transportation from the vendors' point of shipment to and through a California port of entry. The outsourced logistics supplier it selected was Fritz Companies of San Francisco. Fritz specializes in third-party distribution. Its services include customs brokerage, air freight services, ocean freight forwarding, offshore cargo consolidation, ocean transportation as a non-vessel-operating common carrier, and domestic motor, rail and intermodal transportation.

Bill Fehrenbach, Michaels's director of distribution and transportation, explains the company's action as follows:

> We knew we wanted to get back into direct importing, and we knew we didn't want to do it the way we had done it before. We went with Fritz because we wanted some specific service and characteristics they could provide. They have offices in the countries we're doing our buying in. They could provide us with exactly the services we wanted. And they have the system capabilities in place to track our freight and give status reports at any time when it's moving from the vendor to our U.S. port.[6]

Here we have a fine illustration of the value-adding acquisition process at work. Purchasing and logistics are fully integrated, backward to the source and forward to marketing and physical distribution.

- By buying direct, Michaels significantly reduces its cost of product and cost of transporting product.
- By outsourcing transportation to a full-service third-party logistics supplier, it avoids the cost of offshore consolidation, contracting for transportation services, monitoring and tracking shipments, and clearing shipments through customs.
- By ensuring timely and reliable delivery to Michaels' warehouses and distribution centers, it speeds up inventory turnover, increases sales, and improves cash flow.

Admittedly, this is an example of acquisition's taking place within a relatively uncomplicated value network. Michaels's business is a retail business, and its value-adding processes are few and not complex. But there is a lesson to be learned. If we see acquisition as a process that acquires values from outside sources, new areas of opportunity open up. Through integrated procurement and logistics we can increase and enhance value both to internal customers and to outside customers and markets.

Chapter 6

Manufacturing as a Value-Creating Process

Manufacturing is the process that converts materials and components into products and systems. It does this by employing manpower, machines, technology, and information to alter, enhance, reconstitute or recombine them to specific performance or application needs. Manufacturing is a value-creating process when, by this conversion, it satisfies requirements at least customer cost of acquisition, ownership, and use.

As a key process within a company's value network, manufacturing gets the highest visibility in meeting the value challenge. Manufacturing produces—or fails to produce—what customers specify. It meets—or fails to meet—their quality, quantity, and time demands. As we account for manufacturing, it reflects not only the costs it directly incurs but also all costs set in motion by processes employed prior to manufacture. These all show up as costs of product, costs that affect company competitiveness and pricing. This clearly gets higher management attention.

It is this high visibility that makes manufacturing so susceptible to "quick fixes." We're constantly looking for quick and easy solutions to manufacturing problems. Often what we identify as problems are merely manifestations of deeper and more-complex factors.

For example, the drive to improve productivity has led to indiscriminate downsizing through layoffs, attrition, and early retirement incentives. Productivity has risen, but at a price that has yet to be paid. Manufacturing organizations are being decimated. They are losing skilled and experienced manufacturing engineers, plant engineers, and process specialists and managers. Those remaining are often people with less skill and less technical and functional experience.

Because we measure productivity as output per unit of manpower, higher management can gain comfort that downsizing is the answer. But if fewer people are doing nothing more than what was done before—and doing it with less competence—the advantage can be illusory. We're already seeing signs of burnout among technical and supervisory personnel. Many middle managers are now putting in sixty hours a week and more because they're doing the work of two or three positions that were eliminated.

Across-the-board downsizing and reducing staff by some arbitrarily set head count is not the solution to the productivity problem. That solution lies in: (1) understanding how the manufacturing process creates value and how functions and activities contribute to that value-creating process, and (2) modifying the process to be more value effective.

Probably the most dramatic example of an ill-conceived quick fix to manufacturing was General Motors' attempt to automate its Hamtramck facility. The plan was to replace two older Detroit plants building Cadillacs with a single modern one. And the strategy was to employ robotics and computer technology to give Hamtramck the manufacturing competitive edge. Estimates vary as to the exact amount that GM's gamble cost, but all agree it was well into the multibillion-dollar range. And what GM got for its money is described in the following excerpt from a news story appearing in *The Economist*:

> The production lines ground to a halt for hours while technicians tried to debug software. When they did work the robots began dismembering each other, smashing cars, spraying paint everywhere, or even fitting the wrong equipment. Automated Guided Vehicles (AGVs) installed to ferry parts around the factory,

sometimes simply refused to move. What was meant to
be a showcase plant turned into a nightmare.[1]

The "problem" as seen by General Motors management was
how to reduce labor cost to compete more effectively with Japanese automobile manufacturers. Also how to contend with an
aggressive union that did not appear to appreciate the competitive
problem. The "solution" was to automate, to employ robotics in
labor-intensive and low-value-adding manufacturing operations.

The solution chosen was clearly a faulty solution, but that's
because the problem was badly defined. The problem of reducing
labor cost was defined within the context of the company's
existing manufacturing process. Even if they worked as planned,
new machines and robots could improve that process only marginally. They might improve material handling and work flow.
They might even speed them up considerably. But the process
could not turn out defect-free cars, made defect-free the first
time. They could not eliminate—or even reduce—the inventory
that the GM defect-prone process created. Even under the most
favorable of circumstances, so long as the process remained the
same, the benefits of automation would be limited.

After so disastrous an experience, GM learned that its labor-
cost problem was merely a symptom of a larger process problem,
and that automation was not the answer to either. In a case of "if
you can't beat them, join them," General Motors learned this
lesson from Toyota. In 1983, GM and Toyota joined forces in a
venture called New United Motor Manufacturing Inc. (NUMMI).
Its operations were located at an old GM plant in Fremont,
California, and they were put under the management of Toyota.

From its very beginning, NUMMI employed Toyota manufacturing practices and techniques. For example, workers were organized into teams and each team member was trained to perform each task performed by other members. The 200 or so GM
job classifications that previously demarcated one manufacturing
job from another were eliminated. NUMMI also altered the rationale that for years had guided General Motors' manufacturing.
That rationale was to keep assembly lines moving regardless of
the cost. Any defects or failures detected during assembly would

be screened out at the end of the production line and corrected in a rework area. Under the NUMMI management, workers could stop the line at any time to correct assembly faults. The guiding rationale was now "make it right the first time."

Despite misgivings, if not outright opposition from GM managers, the lessons learned at NUMMI were implemented at Hamtramck. Some of the expensive high-tech equipment was removed and replaced by simpler devices to achieve the same results. Workers were organized into working teams. Teams met with parts suppliers to develop ways and means to improve quality. Workers were even encouraged to telephone customers in order to learn firsthand about quality problems and what they might do to prevent them.

This was a radically different approach to manufacturing at General Motors, but it was an approach that paid off. In October of 1991 at the Hamtramck plant in Detroit, the Cadillac Division received the Malcolm Baldrige National Quality Award. This was the first time an automobile company had won that award, and in view of where the division had been five years earlier, this was a remarkable achievement.

Meanwhile, the Toyota techniques were being introduced at General Motors' new subsidiary, the Saturn Corporation, in Spring Hill, Tennessee. Saturn opened in 1990 and incorporated the radical process changes that had proved so effective at NUMMI.

Workers at Saturn are now organized into twelve- to fifteen-member teams. These are self-directed units that do everything from laying out how tasks are to be performed to managing their own budgets, hiring, and inventory control. Teams decide on whether to do work inside or farm it out to subcontractors. They place orders directly to suppliers for tools and parts, without going through more-formal purchase requisitioning procedures. And they do all this with minimal direction from higher management.

Two years after opening its doors, Saturn was producing the highest-quality American car, with defect rates as low as those experienced on Japanese cars. Saturn cars have been a huge success with buyers long disillusioned with past GM products.

Indeed, the Saturns have been so successful that dealers can't keep them in stock. In some locations, the waiting period is three to four months long.

Despite the positive developments at Hamtramck and Saturn, the ultimate jury—the car-buying public—is still out as to whether General Motors has really turned the corner. Years of assembly line manufacturing experience are difficult to shake off. All planning, scheduling, and work-flow controls were designed around that process, and many are still in place. Further, years of managing manufacturing through traditional hierarchical structures make worker-team empowerment a difficult concept to sell.

But the real challenge for General Motors is to develop a deep and compelling sense of manufacturing as a value-creating process rather than a volume-producing one. This has been badly lacking in the past. It has been lacking because the company itself has not been value oriented. Satisfying customer requirements at least cost of ownership and use has not had the highest priority at General Motors. Through its range of products, it has promoted prestige of ownership, aesthetic gratification, or the patriotism in driving a U.S.-built car.

It took the Japanese to demonstrate that what the automobile buyer wanted was steak and not the sizzle. It wanted economy of mileage, reliable performance, and minimal maintenance, all at attractive prices. It took the Japanese to show that supplying what the customer wants beats hands-down supplying what the manufacturer thinks the customer ought to have.

We're Starting From the Wrong End

The world has become a very different place since Henry Ford delivered his oft quoted quip: "The customer can have any color as long as it's black." In Henry's day there weren't that many choices around to enable customers to quibble over color. Cars were so new an experience that buyers were grateful for what they got.

Today, the customer is knowledgeable and fully aware of

choices. He or she is also assertive in demanding that those choices be recognized and met. Customers are no longer that mass market for standardized product selling solely on the basis of low competitive price. They're no longer totally reliant on the manufacturer's technical and marketing sense of what will work and what will sell. And when customers are industrial, commercial, or institutional buyers, those realities apply many times over.

Few managements would dispute these facts. Yet it is surprising how few companies have changed their ways of doing business to adjust to them. This is particularly true among companies that manufacture and sell what they make.

I can't count the number of manufacturing plants I have visited over the years where I have seen the exact same factory layout. It begins with the receiving area at one end of the facility and the shipping dock at the other. Located in between, in invariable juxtaposition, are the stores, machining and subassembly areas, followed by final assembly, painting or finishing, final test and packaging. In bulk chemicals, food processing, and other continuous manufacturing industries, the layout between receiving and shipping accommodates different manufacturing processes, but its design follows essentially the same sequential flow.

More disturbing than our stereotyped factory layout, however, is our stereotyped management thinking. We think about manufacturing in the same step-by-step pattern as our factory layout. We organize people by manufacturing operation and break the operation down by specific task or job designation. We design manufacturing control systems that follow the same work sequencing. But the paradigm for that sequencing is the mass production model. It's a model that assumes a standard product with a long and predictable life and a standard process employing standard machines and equipment. Unfortunately, it's a model that reflects a bygone era. It's a model totally out of touch with the times.

To be successful in today's markets we must rethink our approaches to manufacturing. This means reassessing the advantages and disadvantages of outsourcing rather than making in-house, and it means sharing or leasing physical facilities as against owning them outright. It also means reconsidering plant location in terms of proximity to customers and suppliers, in terms of access to an industrious and skilled work force.

Rethinking manufacturing means reevaluating manufacturing processes and plant design for improved product quality, faster through-put, and enhanced flexibility and turnaround time. And the starting point for this rethinking is the customer. We have to work backward from the customer rather than forward from materials supply. We must determine and define manufacturing processes, physical facilities and layout, and manpower skills on the basis of customer demands and how to best satisfy them.

One would think that this should be self-evident. And if it is, why aren't managements doing more to change their ways? From my experience with scores of companies—large, medium, and small—over the years, I would suggest the following reasons:

1. Managements fail to see manufacturing strategically. They look at it from a short-term, operational perspective. Thus, the strategy that defines business and market planning too often ignores the manufacturing dimension. Manufacturing commands attention only when the strategy must be implemented, and then it's an operational problem.

2. Managements are not always knowledgeable about manufacturing and manufacturing technology. Many senior managers have marketing, financial, or legal backgrounds; relatively few have come up the ranks through manufacturing. So they are ill prepared to evaluate, let alone initiate, radical process changes.

3. The combination of these two factors leads to tunnel vision. Accept the manufacturing process as it basically is. Improve productivity by a new machine or another round of downsizing, but don't tamper with what works—particularly if changing it involves a significant capital investment.

Whether changing our ways involves a capital investment or not, it is imperative that we rethink manufacturing in order to make it a more value-creating process. Customers have become too demanding and technology is too dynamic to assume that how we manufactured in the past will satisfy markets in the future. If foreign competition tells us anything, it's telling us that.

Making It to Order

To appreciate the sea change that has occurred in manufacturing technology from the days of Henry Ford, consider the following. When Ford switched over from producing the Model T to the Model A, his plants were shut down for five months to accomplish the changeover. Today we learn that researchers are working with Japanese automobile manufacturers towards a long-term goal of a "three-day car." According to a *Business Week* story, the aim is to engineer cars around interchangeable components and assemblies: engines, bodies, transmissions, brake and power systems. By mixing and matching these, customers could literally buy cars to their own specification. And they could expect their built-to-order cars to be delivered in three days.[2]

Whether we ever get to see a "three-day car," the fact is that customizing or building products to customer order is a reality. It's a reality even in industries that are conventionally seen as mass producing. Personal-computer manufacturing is a case in point.

Dell Computer is a major producer of IBM-compatible PCs. It assembles these from commercially available components in what *The Economist* called a "motley collection of factory buildings."[3] Manufacturing is done by twelve-worker assembly teams. At Dell's Austin, Texas, plant, each team can produce a fully configured machine, ready for testing in about nine minutes. In a *Computer Reseller News* interview, Dell's production manager, Steve Smith, said that with its six assembly lines the company is able to produce 1,000 to 1,500 systems—the vast majority customer configured—per eight-hour shift.[4]

Incidentally, in referring to Dell's "motley collection of factory buildings" *The Economist* also noted that Dell employs minimal automation. It believes that people are more flexible than machines.[5] So, customizing does not necessarily mean robots and costly manufacturing control systems.

NCR has taken a slightly different route than Dell in customizing product. The recent AT&T acquisition has installed a semi-automated assembly line to satisfy the demand of its computer reseller market. A primary concern of resellers is product availability. NCR now addresses that concern by preconfiguring PCs and work stations to reseller-expressed preferences. Bruce Langos, NCR's assistant vice president of stragetic planning, describes the change as follows:

> The program includes building standard configurations, based on reseller suggestions, that are likely to yield high volume sales. We'll also build base platforms to be specially configured on an assembly line for nonstandard computers. For systems integrators that need special networking . . . we're implementing processes that will provide built-to-order systems more quickly than before.[6]

NCR hopes to cut lead times on nonstandard machines and systems to as low as forty-eight hours instead of five to ten days. On specially configured systems for integrators, lead times are now within ten days rather than the fifteen to sixteen days it took before.

The two examples I've cited demonstrate changes in the manufacturing process to make it more customer responsive. Those changes did not take place out of altruism—not even enlightened altruism. They were driven by demands of the market, a market unique in the following five respects.

1. The PC industry is highly competitive. It is bitterly competitive on price, but also competitive on product performance, product availability, and after-sale service.
2. Technology is changing rapidly. The combination of higher-performance microchips, disk drives, and compatible software is obsoleting product at a faster and faster rate.
3. Despite its technology, the product has become a commodity. Components are commercially available and eas-

ily assembled so that literally hundreds of suppliers can and do produce PCs.
4. Differentiating PCs and avoiding pure price competition means configuring components to achieve customer-desired performance and reliability levels.
5. The market is extremely knowledgeable and sophisticated. Customers know what they want and they'll shop around to make sure they get it.

It is this combination of market factors that has shaped the manufacturing process at Dell and NCR. Indeed, it has shaped the manufacturing process of manufacturers not only in PCs but in workstations, laptop and mainframe computers, printers, and fax and copying machines. It will shape the manufacturing process in all industries facing similar market conditions.

The distinguishing feature of this changed manufacturing process is that it's essentially final assembly and test. Final assembly may be through the twelve-worker assembly-team approach employed at Dell, or through a semiautomated production line as at NCR. The explanation for the difference in the two approaches lies again in the difference in markets served.

Eighty-five percent of Dell's computers are sold over the telephone. Half of these are sold to individual customers, and all are built to order. Dell is successful in this market because it is highly price competitive. It aims for a net profit margin of only 5 percent. Therefore, the company avoids the high fixed costs that automation would entail.

NCR, on the other hand, has concentrated on the resale market—the value-added reseller (VAR) and the systems integrator. These customers sell NCR's products in conjunction with their technical services. They sell solutions first and hardware as a means of achieving that solution. Their priorities are product reliability and availability; low price is secondary. And their hardware needs are more generic than specific. So automating part of the assembly process makes good sense for NCR.

Regardless of the approach, the reasoning behind a process of final assembly and test is the same. Avoiding fabrication of parts and subassemblies simplifies the manufacturing process. It reduces work loads, plant and equipment, manpower and management requirements. This simplification ripples backward through purchasing and engineering, which improves the integration of these processes with manufacturing.

Final-assembly manufacturing reduces inventory line items. This reduces carrying costs and improves inventory turnover. It reduces or eliminates warehousing and storage space, machine and tool maintenance, machine setup and tool changeover. But most importantly, final-assembly manufacturing provides flexibility. By mixing and matching components to meet specific customer demand, the process is highly customer responsive. It's also responsive within a highly compressed manufacturing time cycle.

The Flexible Factory

Years before it was acquired by United Technologies, I consulted with the Carrier Corporation. Over a three-year period I visited air-conditioning and compressor plants in New York, Pennsylvania, Texas, California, and Tennessee. In each location, manufacturing was the same large-volume-oriented process, with dedicated machines and assembly lines all geared to turning out a standard product or line of product continuously.

With that recollection in mind, it was a pleasant surprise to learn how the company had changed. The *Wall Street Journal* ran a feature article on Carrier's new compressor plant in Arkadelphia, Arkansas. According to the *Journal*, the plant maintains no finished-goods inventory because it makes compressors only to order. Compressors are the most critical and costly component of an air conditioner. They represent as much as 50 percent of product cost, and making them to order is a radical change from how they were produced in the past.

When I worked with Carrier, compressors were built to forecast. Based on estimated air-conditioner sales, Carrier would project compressor requirements and produce and purchase them to meet forecast. Unfortunately, forecasts were constantly changing, and as they changed, production schedules changed.

The only buffer for manufacturing against the impact of those changes was large safety stocks of finished goods, raw materials, and work in process. So the Carrier facilities I remember had extensive storage and warehouse areas. And a large part of the work force was employed in handling, storing, and moving materials and product at every stage of the manufacturing process.

At Arkadelphia, the process is highly automated. The *Journal* describes one operation as follows: "The person places two pieces of metal in a cutting machine, shuts the glass doors and punches a button. Guided by a computer that keeps the cut from straying more than 8 millionths of an inch, the machine slices steel like butter."[7]

In the old Carrier compressor plants I visited, steel cutting was not computer aided. It involved multiple machining steps performed by multiple machine operators. And the tolerances held were closer to eight one-hundredths of an inch than to eight one-millionths.

The Arkadelphia plant, however, is a model of efficiency and aesthetic appeal. It's a one-story structure with clusters of automated equipment, designed and arrayed for maximum flexibility. It is spotlessly clean, and quiet enough for you to "hear a whisper" on the factory floor. The *Journal* says it looks more like an insurance office than a factory. But most surprisingly, it employs only 150 people. That's a small fraction of the work force in the Carrier plants I remember.

The compressor manufacturing process combines automation and worker empowerment to achieve a high degree of flexibility. Workers are trained to perform several jobs, so that if one worker is absent, another can fill in quickly. The first employees hired at Arkadelphia visited the machine-tool supplier building the plant equipment and learned how to install the equipment themselves. Because of that experience they can fix machines on their own, should a breakdown occur.

Workers can shut down production if they detect a problem. They can order supplies on their own without going through formal requisitioning. Instead of being supervised in the traditional factory foreman-to-worker mode, worker teams supervise themselves. They learn who in the team has which skills and take direction from the most knowledgeable.

Arkadelphia's immediate customer is Carrier's air-conditioning units. And in terms of satisfying customer requirements, the plant's manufacturing meets every criterion of a value-creating process. It supplies high-quality compressors, an essential feature of reliable and energy-efficient air conditioners. It delivers them on a build-to-order, just-in-time basis. It produces them at a cost lower than they've been produced before and $35 per unit lower than the company pays to buy them from outside suppliers.

Whether the plant is a model for future plants is difficult to say. It now produces a single line of product, for a single application. And its primary customers are the air-conditioning units of the parent Carrier corporation. Yet, both plant and equipment were designed for maximum flexibility. It is possible that the process could be adapted to produce a new or modified product mix or be adjusted to satisfy a different customer base. Carrier's Compressor Division president, Thomas L. Lassouf, says: "The whole plant could probably be reconfigured in several weeks." He has also said, "My goal is to sell compressors from Arkansas to Japan."[8]

Small Is Beautiful

It is evident that mass-production processes are increasingly irrelevant in today's markets. Markets are now geographically dispersed, they are highly fragmented, they demand product diversity and special tailoring to meet unique and changing requirements. Manufacturing monoliths geared to grinding out volumes of standard product are an anachronism.

What is evolving to supply today's markets are flexible or agile manufacturing systems. These are systems employed by small to medium companies that have identified a market niche and structured their manufacturing process to satisfy it. Or, they're employed by larger multiproduct companies that have broken down their manufacturing operations into small, specialized units to better serve a more closely defined customer base.

We have already described one approach to flexible manufacturing through confining the process to final assembly and test. The process may involve worker teams organized into assembly units with little automation, as is the case at Dell Computer. Or it may be a semiautomated process, combining materials handling and transfer systems along with worker teams, as I described at NCR.

This pattern for achieving flexibility works well in markets that are volatile or susceptible to rapid technological change. Its short manufacturing cycle time allows for quick response to changing customer demand. Its reliance on outside-supplied components rather than internally manufactured ones makes it quick and easy to incorporate advanced design features into final product.

Carrier's manufacturing process, on the other hand, is suited to a different type of market. At its compressor plant, it produces a limited line of product for a limited customer base. It may be incorrect to label it a captive customer base, but it is a relatively stable one. Compressor manufacturing does not entail rapid technological change. It involves basic components like coils, dampers, and blades that lend themselves to automated manufacturing methods. Assembly of components to final-product design is through worker assembly teams. Empowering teams to be self-directing speeds up cycle times and improves product quality. It also makes assembly quick to adapt to fluctuating customer order quantities and rates.

For companies in cyclical markets with a wide customer base, flexible manufacturing is achieved through processes that group specially designed machines into work cells. These are manufacturing modules integrated to produce a common family of product or to perform a common sequence of operations. While some companies have invested heavily in large-scale automation—some even pursuing fully automated manufacturing from raw materials to finished product—others have employed this more measured approach with good success.

Deere and Company is the largest manufacturer of agricultural equipment in the world. Yet it has had to contend with increasingly intense competition, particularly from foreign producers. To meet competition, the company sped up new-product introdution. It drastically changed its manufacturing processes to improve its ability to respond to customer demands. Modular manufacturing was the choice it adopted.

Under its traditional methods of manufacture, Deere machined every part going into every product on machines specifically designed for a specific operation: cutting, drilling, grinding. Both machines and workers were dedicated to producing the same part repetitively. More than a decade ago, Deere recognized the limitations of that approach. It was too constraining; it was not adaptable to change. To introduce new products rapidly, and to cater to specific customer preferences, the manufacturing processes had to be redesigned.

In 1981 Deere began a massive program of reengineering manufacturing. It set up twelve flexible machining centers at its factory complex in Waterloo, Iowa. These were totally automated and computer-directed manufacturing units. Each unit simultaneously produced four varieties of transmission cases for five new tractor models. Equipped with as many as sixty tools, each machining center was capable of a wide range of machining tasks. They could machine a single family of tractor parts or be easily programmed to produce a wider combination of parts and products. They also accommodated changes in design with minimum delay. Where it had taken months to implement design changes under the old methods of manufacture, it now took Deere only a matter of hours under its flexibile manufacturing approach.

Companies can achieve flexibility on a smaller scale. They can employ versatile machines in machine cells to produce a common variety of parts. This is done by stationing machines around a parts-handling system. The system is typically computer controlled and has automated tool changeover capability. This gives cells continuing flexibility to handle new parts as they come out of design, even to handle design changes. Machining cells include the fixturing, special tooling, and special equipment required to produce the assigned family of parts. This makes them self-contained manufacturing entities, which reduces waiting and transfer time to a minimum.

For small manufacturing operations, flexibility can be

achieved with stand-alone machines that work like cells because they're palletized. A palletized cell is created when a two-pallet single-machine process is linked through the pallets to other machines. While one pallet is loaded and moved into place, the other pallet with finished parts is transferred to another machine in the process flow. By integrating stand-alone machines into machining cells, manufacturing can develop into a more automated process, one cell at a time.

What allows manufacturing to achieve the flexibility today's markets demand is the advancements we've achieved in manufacturing technology. The list of these achievements is impressive—computer-assisted design and manufacturing systems (CAD/CAM), computer numerically controlled machines, versatile machines, robotics, lasers and fiber optics, sensors, automated material-handling systems and transfer lines, and all of the software packages that store, retrieve, integrate, and process machine instructions and data.

Clearly, we can't afford to incorporate all these advancements; nor would we want to if we could. Some don't contribute customer value commensurate with their cost. Others do so only marginally. But we can be selective in what we employ to make manufacturing more flexible, more responsive to market and technology demands. And again the place to begin is with the customer.

Demand Pull, Not Supply Push

Flexible manufacturing is not an end in itself; it is a means to an end. That end is precisely the one we pursue through techniques known as "total quality" and "just-in-time": to satisfy market and customer requirements cost-effectively.

Unfortunately, we can look at these techniques as reflecting three separate and distinct management concepts. Indeed, we can even look at them as competing, if not conflicting, concepts. This is apt to happen when we become so immersed in their individual methodology that we forget their common objective. Flexible manufacturing, total quality and just-in-time are a trinity of concepts reflecting an all-embracing one: managing for value results.

Toyota, which systematized just-in-time, defines it as the "reduction of cost through the elimination of waste." Waste is any excess of time, material, facilities, or human resources. So JIT is not only a technique for reducing cost; necessarily, it's a technique for improving quality.

Meanwhile, total quality stresses making it right the first time—preventing defects and failures to avoid correcting for them later. By definition, that's also eliminating waste. Thus, total quality and just-in-time are complementary techniques aimed at the same results.

But to implement these techniques invariably requires fundamental changes in the manufacturing process. Process changes, however, are dictated by the demands of the market, and market demands are constantly changing. So to ensure total quality and to ensure just-in-time, the process must be a flexible one.

Flexible manufacturing is merely tailoring the manufacturing process to achieve quality and time objectives. As such, it is the third leg of a three-legged manufacturing management stool. Together with total quality and just-in-time techniques, it is what makes manufacturing a value-creating process. Ignoring any one leg, or emphasizing one at the expense of the others, produces the same result as any one- or two-legged stool: It collapses.

JIT has been described as a "demand pull" manufacturing technique. This means that we make only what is required, when it is required. We assemble final product in the quantity and at the time to satisfy market demand. We fabricate parts for assembly only as they are required for assembly. Demand pulls production.

"Supply push" is the opposite approach. Materials supply pushes parts fabrication, parts supply pushes final assembly, and inevitably final assembly pushes sales. We sell—or try to sell— what we've made. If we can't do it at one price, we lower the price or write off the inventory.

The "demand pull" rationale in just-in-time is manifest also in the total-quality technique. Customer specification or market demand are the starting points for product-quality definition. Actual customer experience then pulls the effort for quality improvement. Customer rejections and field service repairs identify the nature and frequency of product failure. This pulls the problem-solving process of pinpointing causes and seeking possible solutions. The optimal solution pulls corrective action in product design, manufacturing process, or supplier manufacturing and quality control.

Just as customer or market demand are the force that pulls time and quality effort, they are also the force that pulls manufacturing into a more flexible process mode. It's the market that fashions the manufacturing process. And how it's fashioned reflects the precise nature of how the market behaves. Is technology changing rapidly, and do customers demand continuing product enhancement? Are markets unstable, with sharp expansions and contractions in demand occurring in short time intervals? Are customers competing on product differentiation, so that what we produce is dictated by their need to innovate? These are critical questions concerning market and customer requirements. And working backward from that starting point, we design or redesign manufacturing to be a more adaptable and flexible value process.

In fashioning that process the kinds of questions we need to explore are ones like the following:

- Which tasks and operations in the process are best performed internally, and which are best farmed out? The fact that we now perform them in-house is not a good answer. Are they quality-, time-, and cost-effective? If not, outsource them.
- Which machine or worker operations have high defect or failure rates? What is their nature and frequency? How are they caused and what can we do to prevent them?
- Which manufacturing areas generate bottlenecks during production? Is it order processing? materials handling? machine setup or changeover time? How do we avoid or eliminate the bottlenecks?
- Which machines and which operations in the process show

the lowest uptime or the lowest productivity? Where do we have breakdowns, excessive waiting times, or delays? Why?

- Which operations show poor synchronizing between machine and worker? Is one faster or slower than the other, or out of phase with the other? How do we smooth out their interaction?
- Which operations are badly synchronized? Are they out-of-time phasing or volume phasing? Again, why?
- Which operations are cost contributors but not value contributors—that is, they add nothing to customer satisfaction? How can we eliminate them, reduce them, or combine them for cost-effectiveness? Handling, inspection, and transfer activities, which are common to most manufacturing processes, are prime candidates to consider.
- Above all, how can we simplify the process and make it a more flexible, failure-free process that satisfies customer quality, time, and cost demands?

What Does It Take to Get There?

Business journals tend to publish stories built around some popular theme or some well-known company. And so over the past few years, we have seen endless stories about total quality management (TQM), just-in-time (JIT), and flexible manufacturing. Each of these concepts is presented as a distinctive management technique, related only by inference to other techniques. And more often than not, the companies chosen to illustrate them are large corporations.

To begin with, TQM, JIT, and flexible manufacturing are integral elements of a broader concept, the concept of satisfying customer requirements cost-effectively. When implemented through manufacturing, they make manufacturing a value-creating process. That is true for all companies, small or large. Indeed, the large companies that are described as practitioners of these value-adding techniques are typically organized into smaller, decentralized manufacturing units. Hence, when a Hewlett-Packard, a General Electric, or a Xerox are cited for excellence in manufacturing, it is always a particular division, department, or operating unit that is cited. This puts the example into the same size and volume range of small- to medium-size companies. So these value-adding techniques have universal, not limited, application.

Small or large, there is no pat formula for determining what makes a manufacturing company successful. However, I'd suggest that there are traits and characteristics that distinguish companies that view manufacturing as a value-creating process from those that don't:

1. They are market driven and are guided by the market as to how they manufacture. Their manufacturing processes follow the identification of the market to be served, not the other way around.

2. They are small by mass-production standards. Thirty to 300 people is the size of most manufacturing operations that employ value-adding techniques, with the majority of them in the 100- to 200-people range.

3. Their forte is customizing products to specific customer application. Customizing can be mass customizing, as we see in desktop-computer manufacturing, or the one-of-a-kind design and build of a machine tool.

4. The mix of process equipment, physical layout, and people skills is designed for flexibility, high quality, and quick response time. It is not designed to minimize unit labor costs.

5. They keep a tight lid on manufacturing overheads. From avoiding low-value-contributing labor in handling, storing, and moving materials to minimizing setup, inspection, and supervision, they are lean producers.

6. They are highly selective in the people they recruit. Workers at high-value-adding plants are better educated than the lunch-pail crews who manned yesterday's mass-production lines. They're team players; yet they show a high degree of personal initiative. And with these attri-

butes, management empowers them to be self-directed and self-monitored.

7. They stress customer service and customer satisfaction. The link between manufacturing and the customer is infinitely more direct in value-added manufacturing plants than it was even in the best-managed mass-production operations.

8. They are functionally integrated and compose a tightly knit value network. Manufacturing and marketing, manufacturing and engineering are not "us" and "them." Like their work teams on the factory floor, all functions and processes work together for common objectives.

9. They avoid competing on price. As niche players they seek high-margin rather than high-volume business. Of course, there are exceptions, but high quality, quick response time, and flexible manufacturing allow market and customer selectivity. It would be a waste not to exploit that fact.

10. They are led by bright and imaginative managements who understand manufacturing as a value-creating process, who are enterprising and gutsy enough to make necessary changes whenever the process requires them.

Chapter 7

Value and the Customer Service Process

I didn't plan it this way, but as I started writing this chapter on customer service, I had a real-life experience that exemplified the lack of it.

This past Christmas I received a hi-fi camcorder as a gift from my son. It came with an enhanced zoom lens, and to prevent scratching or other damage, I decided to purchase a protective lens cover. The printed material that accompanied the camcorder gave an 800 number to order accessories or replacement parts. It all seemed so convenient and simple. As things turned out, it was neither.

To begin with, I had to go through the ritual of those annoying telephone instructions: "If you are dialing from a Touch-tone phone press 1 for whatever; press 2, 3, or 4 for whatever else." After making my choice—which was not all that easy—I heard that inevitable recorded message: "Our operators are all busy with other customers. Please stay on the line for the next available representative."

Three minutes go by. Again that voice: "We value your call, so please stay on the line. The next available representative will be with you shortly." Five minutes go by, ten minutes go by: the same recording. All this time I'm serenaded by the background sounds of Beethoven's *Pastoral* Symphony. Lovely music, but it can't soothe my growing rage. Finally, after eighteen minutes I hear a human voice. Pleasant it is not; understanding it is less. The fact that I have waited nearly twenty minutes to talk to someone she finds "really surprising." But I "must understand" I'm not the only person calling—they're "busy with other customers."

The coup de grace, however, is that they don't stock protective lens covers at this location. Further, my "Service Representative" has no idea where I might call to order one. Needless to say, I got my cover elsewhere; but also needless to say, I was a most unhappy caller.

From my discussions with countless people in all walks of life on the subject, I'm sure my experience was not unique. Indeed, there is ample evidence to prove it is more the norm than the exception.

Learning International is a worldwide leader in training for business, industry, and government. Prior to its being acquired by the Times-Mirror Company, it was part of the Xerox Corporation and was called Xerox Learning Systems. Recently, it published a study on customer satisfaction in which it cites surveys by Louis Harris and the American Society of Quality Control. Those surveys show that "The American public believes the quality of most products and services has declined and will continue to decline. In fact, as many as three out of four people believe products and services just aren't what they need to be."[1]

In a similar vein, a Washington, D.C.–based consulting group known as Technical Assistance Research Programs Institute (TARPI) conducted a study of customer service for the Consumer Affairs Office in the White House. It found that 95 percent of the customers who had a bad buying experience never bothered to file complaints. They never filed because they expected little or no satisfaction. However, 91 percent of those customers also refused to go back. Moreover, the study found that the average dissatisfied customer related his or her dissatisfaction to nine to ten other people. As a footnote, the study showed that it costs five times as much to get a new customer as it does to satisfy an existing one.[2]

With such disturbing findings about poor service and its consequences, it's surprising that we don't see real improvement. Admittedly, there is a growing awareness of the problem. Hardly a day goes by that we don't read about "King Customer" and "Focusing on Customer Satisfaction." And increasingly, companies are touting customer service as a "marketplace distinguisher," a source of "competitive advantage," a "profit strategy." But for the most part, the results have not measured up to the sloganizing.

Whither Customer Service?

In the simplest of terms, customer service is that set of activities that ensures customer satisfaction with company product or service offerings. As such it involves tasks performed before an order is taken, throughout its production/delivery cycle, and after delivery is made. Thus, it embodies marketing, engineering, acquisition/logistics, and manufacturing activities in a continuous value-adding and value-ensuring process. Of all the processes employed in an operating business, none epitomizes the network paradigm more than customer service. And none more directly reflects the concept of value as the satisfaction of customer requirements at least cost of acquisition, ownership, and use.

Herein lies the reason for the lack of real improvement. Few companies view customer service in these terms. Most see customer service as an ancillary activity of other processes rather than a value-contributing process in its own right.

In some companies it's limited to handling customer orders and dealing with customer complaints. These are considered marketing or sales activities. In other companies, customer service is equated with on-time delivery, and ensuring delivery is a manufacturing or distribution activity. In still other companies, customer service means providing technical assistance and support, an engineering activity. In each of these instances, customer service is defined in narrow functional terms with no common rationale to make for a unifying and cohesive process.

Clearly, the scope and importance of customer service will

vary by industry and by companies that make up an industry. At one extreme it may be limited in scope and of relatively small importance. This is the case for discount retailers selling nationally advertised consumer goods out of bare-bones shopping facilities. At the other extreme it may be extensive in scope and critical. Companies supplying custom-built components to OEM customers competing in volatile or technically demanding markets fall into this category.

Customer Service Is Implied

Customer service is an implied customer requirement. Unlike quality, quantity, and time requirements, it is rarely specified. What determines its scope and importance are customer expectations and customer perceptions of its worth in value terms. How does it satisfy requirements that, though not specified, are still acknowledged? How does it affect customer cost?

For example, in the case of discount retailers like Costco and the Price Club, selling primarily on the basis of low price, customers don't expect individualized attention. They're not turned off by warehouse-type facilities where shoppers pick from racks and skids and carry their purchases to a checkout station. They place greater comparative worth on low price than the convenience and comfort of being served in more-personalized and -pleasing surroundings.

In the case of suppliers of custom-built components like Eaton or Honeywell, selling in volatile or technically demanding OEM markets, customers expect and can command a wide array of services. They range from application engineering to inventory stocking and replenishment programs, to after-sale product and technical support.

What determines the scope and importance of customer service is the nature of the market. What do customers demand? What does competition provide? Without question, as customers become more knowledgeable and assertive, their demands for improved customer service will accelerate. And as competition becomes more creative and aggressive, the penalty for not providing improved service will be loss of market.

As a value-adding, value-ensuring process, customer service comprises the following areas of activity:

1. *Presale communication and customer assistance, which includes*:
   - Handling customer inquiries
   - Developing and providing specifications
   - Quoting prices and availability
   - Providing sales and delivery terms
2. *Order entry, including*:
   - Taking orders for products and services
   - Editing customer orders
   - Processing changes to customer orders
   - Tracing order status
3. *Handling claims and credits, which deals with*:
   - Resolving customer complaints
   - Processing customer rejections and returns
4. *Logistics support, which includes the tracking of*:
   - Quality-control performance
   - Production-planning and inventory-control performance
   - Inventory warehouse and transportation operations
5. *Maintenance, repair, and disposal, including*:
   - Preventive maintenance
   - Spares and replacement inventory support
   - Disposition of surplus and obsolete product

These activities combine to make up three subprocesses of customer service:

1. *Information exchange*, which includes the two-way transfer of information and data leading up to customer order placement, through order filling, and after-order completion.
2. *Performance monitoring and logistics support*, which oversees supplier production and logistics performance in meeting customer quality and delivery requirements.

3. *Customer satisfaction guarantee,* which includes product and
   service warranties and administering after-sale repair, replacement, and credits.

Information Exchange: The Lifeblood of Customer Service

We have described business as a network of value-contributing
processes. In an analogy between the physiological network of
the human body and the business network, we could liken
business processes to the body's functioning systems: the cardio-
vascular system, the gastrointestinal system, the respiratory system. As blood flow provides the means of sustaining life to these
bodily systems, information flow provides the means of sustaining the effectiveness of business processes. And to none is this
analogy more applicable than the customer service process.

From the first to the last contact, information circulates in a
continuous exchange between customer and supplier. It covers
every facet of customer concern: product specifications, price and
delivery, order status. It covers every facet of supplier concern:
order quantities, schedule due dates, customer assessments of
supplier quality and delivery performance.

Fortunately, the advancements we've made in information
technology enable us to handle this exchange better than we ever
did before. Unfortunately, however, its scope and volume are so
large that we handle it in a fragmented fashion, with little cohesiveness from one area of application to another.

Further, the systems that provide the data for information
exchange are not designed for customer service. They're designed to plan and manage inventories, control manufacturing
operations, schedule and monitor the logistics of inbound and
outbound materials and product flow. The focus of these systems
is internally directed to promote efficiency in their operation, cost
containment or improvement in their performance. When the
data these systems provide are employed in customer information exchange, they must be extracted and organized specifically
for that task. This makes that exchange a piecemeal process,

which limits its effectiveness in providing meaningful customer support.

Electronic Data Interchange

Information systems that link customers and suppliers electronically are known as electronic data interchange. EDI systems have been around for years, but their employment as a strategic tool of customer service has been slow to develop. That's because in most cases EDI was initiated not by companies to implement marketing objectives but by their customers to implement purchasing objectives. It was imposed on suppliers to shorten the purchasing cycle and reduce the paperwork flow.

Texas Instruments, for example, purchases about $3.8 billion of materials a year. Half of all the purchase orders it generates are EDI transactions. These are with those 900 of the company's 14,000 suppliers who are tied in electronically through TI buyer workstations. Through these computers, buyers request quotations from preapproved suppliers, place purchase orders, and monitor order status. They can learn what other TI purchasers pay for common commodities, as well as check on supplier quality and delivery ratings as measured by all TI divisions.

Texas Instruments began using EDI in 1979 with about fifty suppliers. It was a primitive E-mail system used primarily for teletyping purchase orders. In the 1980s, TI developed a more sophisticated system, which allowed buyers to communicate and negotiate with suppliers about price, delivery, and quantity.

To be tied into the system as an on-line source, however, demanded, and still demands, that suppliers have a dedicated computer programmed with TI proprietary software for that purpose. So in a very real sense Texas Instruments defines the mode and content of information exchange it expects from its suppliers. Whether those suppliers acknowledge the fact or not, this makes that exchange an activity of their customer's acquisition process rather than an activity of their own customer service process.

Another example of this is seen at General Motors' Truck and

Bus Division. Electronic Data Systems (EDS), GM's data-management subsidiary, worked with the product division to develop a factory control system. Part of that system included the application of electronic data interchange to the purchase and receipt of all production material. EDS and the division together determined the requirements suppliers would have to meet in order to be approved as EDI sources. As suppliers demonstrated their ability to meet those requirements, they were certified for EDI transactions in the GM-EDS mode.

The Truck and Bus Division does not only place purchase orders electronically; it does a great deal more. Through EDI it transmits its unloading schedule to suppliers, who then transmit back an advanced shipping notification the moment trucks leave their shipping dock. Raw materials like steel are bar coded. At receiving, an employee reads the bar code using a radio-frequency device. This provides instant information on specification compliance, order fill rates, and availability to production for further processing. But again, the mode and content of EDI is determined by General Motors, the customer.

In and of itself this is not bad. After all, customer service must be customer oriented. But the point is that important elements of information exchange now reflect customer acquisition objectives and priorities, rather than supplier strategy for providing customer service. This poses the danger that a customer-dictated EDI system could limit a supplier's ability to implement more-meaningful information exchange with other customers.

Certainly it means that suppliers must be selective about the customers whose EDI systems become the operative systems. Those customers should be ones who are major accounts and with whom suppliers have established long-term partnering-type relationships. With other customers the risks can well outweigh the rewards. This can be a particular problem for component manufacturers selling in multichannel OEM markets. Here, conforming to a customer's EDI requirements may mean doing business on a competitor's terms and conditions of purchase. It may mean loss of data confidentiality to a current or prospective competitor.

An Alternative Approach

An industry that has had more success in structuring EDI systems to reflect marketing and customer service strategies is the electronics distribution industry. This is probably because electronics distributors sell to a large number of customers, no single one accounting for a significant share of the total business. Their business is buying and reselling, with little engineering or manufacturing intervening. Thus, they can fashion a customer information exchange system in two ways:

1. On a broad base of common buying practice and procedure
2. With a common logic of information content and flow to serve both their acquisition and marketing/customer service objectives

Arrow Electronics, one of the largest electronic distributors, provides a good case example. Arrow conducts its day-to-day business with both suppliers and customers via electronic data interchange. With almost 3,000 terminals on-line nationwide, it receives up-to-date information on product availability, lead times, pricing, and technical specifications. Arrow's sales representatives can instantly access the system for that same information either to transmit to customers or to place orders, expedite shipments, or request additional data.

In many cases, customers have Arrow terminals installed at their sites. They are found in purchasing and engineering offices so that customer personnel can access desired information themselves. They can also order directly without going through a lengthy requisition/purchase-order procedure.

In a typical EDI relationship, Arrow's mainframe computer electronically exchanges purchase orders, invoices, and remittances with a customer's mainframe, eliminating time-consuming paperwork and increasing accuracy and speed in handling purchasing details. John Smith, Arrow's vice president of manufacturing information systems, says: "We are committed to EDI because it allows us to completely automate the purchasing function, whether with suppliers or customers. EDI allows us to react much more quickly to inventory demands, and at the same time helps our customers eliminate unnecessary costs."[3]

EDI Standards

One of the factors limiting the application of electronic data interchange to more strategically oriented customer service has been the lack of uniform standards. Different industries and even different companies have established their own standards. Thus, unless suppliers have superior leverage in their customer-supplier relationship, they either conform to the customer's EDI system or run the risk of being nonapproved sources.

Without question, this can limit the number of customer suppliers. But that is often a small price to pay for the advantages of doing business through an information exchange system designed specifically for purchasing purposes.

There is however a growing trend toward acceptance of standards set by the American National Standards Institute (ANSI). Identified as X–12 standards, they are structured so that computer programs can translate data from internal to external formats. This provides a common language for exchanging data between customers and suppliers. The information covered by these standards relates to transactions like requests for quotations, purchase-order placement and acknowledgement, receiving advice and shipping schedules. These are all purchasing-related transactions, but obviously they are also the information exchange demands imposed on the customer service process.

Figure 7-1 shows a list of the transactions covered by these standards, with their corresponding ANSI designations. Increasingly, both customers and their suppliers are modifying their information systems to reflect these standards. Customers are doing so to increase the number of preapproved sources in their supply base. Suppliers are doing so because the market and competition demand it. The more information exchange systems reflect common EDI standards, the more they can be tailored to implement customer service objectives.

Figure 7-1.   Accredited standards committee X-12 standards of the
American National Standards Institute.

.810	Invoice X 12.2
.820	Payment Order/Remittance Advice X 12.4
.830	Planning Schedule with Release Capability
.832	Price/Sale Catalog X 12.13
.840	Request for Quotation X 12.7
.843	Response to Request for Quotation X 12.8
.845	Price Authorization Acknowledgement/Status X 12.27
.850	Purchase Order X 12.1
.855	Purchase Order Acknowledgement X 12.9
.856	Ship Notice/Manifest X 12.10
.860	Purchase Order Change X 12.15
.861	Receiving Advice X 12.12
.862	Shipping Schedule X 12.37
.863	Report of Test Results X 12.41
.865	Purchase Order Change Acknowledgement X 12.16
.867	Order Status Inquiry X 12.12
.870	Order Status Report X 12.23

Clearly, even the most comprehensive EDI system cannot encompass the full extent of customer information exchange. Much of that exchange still demands personal contact and dialogue. However, if the EDI system is carefully structured, it can achieve an important objective of the customer service process: the creation and implementation of a "hassle-free" customer order. This is no small accomplishment. Some of the more common causes of customer complaint are errors or delays in that process: errors in order entry, missing product or specification information, incomplete documentation, pricing and invoice errors, lack of timely notice of product availability, order status, or shipping dates. These all make for customer dissatisfaction; these all increase customer cost.

Performance Monitoring and Logistics Support

I've defined *customer service* as that set of activities which ensures customer satisfaction with company product and service offerings. In this sense, customer service is a total company effort. It is the consequence of company dedication to customer value. It is the result of company success in integrating value-contributing processes to satisfy customer quality, quantity, and time demands.

In the context of day-to-day operations, however, customer service is also a more specifically focused process. It is a process involving the monitoring of company product and production performance. It is the process of providing the logistics support to satisfy customer demands as and when they arise.

TQM-JIT and Logistics Support

Total quality management (TQM) and just-in-time (JIT) are two management methods aimed at improving company product and production performance. Total quality management is the application of statistical methods and human resources to meet quality requirements the first time and every time, with minimum variance. Just-in-time is a method of synchronizing production with demand so that manufacturing and supply take place only as demand requires.

Both TQM and JIT are designed to reduce cost through the elimination of waste—waste in the form of product defects, waste in the form of excess inventory. TQM and JIT are interrelated and interacting. The objectives of one cannot be achieved without the other. And together, they provide a vital discipline for providing and improving customer satisfaction.

The role of customer service in implementing TQM and JIT is twofold. First, it is to monitor quality and production through customer feedback on product and delivery performance. Second, it is to forge logistics links between company and customer, so that quality and delivery requirements are satisfied more reliably and at lower customer cost of acquisition, ownership, and use.

Performance monitoring takes many forms. It's identifying and quantifying the nature and frequency of product failures reflected in customer rejections and returns. It's following up progress on customer orders and tracking fill rates and delivery dates on those orders. Feedback on performance comes from many sources. It comes from customer complaints, salesperson calls, customer surveys, and focus groups.

Performance monitoring guided and supported by customer feedback provides the most reliable basis for achieving and maintaining customer satisfaction.

FORD MOTOR COMPANY, badly hurt by Japanese competition, convened a focus group of California buyers in 1980 to evaluate Ford cars. According to a *Business Week* story, what Ford heard from that group was shocking. The general consensus was that Ford had let its customers down. This was particularly true among older people. Among the younger people, the sentiment was that no one wanted a Ford, that many had never been in a Ford, and that few knew anyone who owned a Ford.[4]

Prompted into action by what it heard, Ford sped up development of its Taurus and Sable models. Design engineers solicited suggestions from additional consumer groups. They sought consumer evaluations of prototype designs. These resulted in design features on the Taurus like a sloped floor under the rear seats to provide more foot room, a widened space between the seat adjustment tracks, tracks made out of smooth plastic instead of metal.

Ford now surveys some 2.5 million customers a year and regularly invites owners to meet with engineers and dealers to discuss quality problems.

DETROIT DIESEL, a producer of truck engines, was for years a money-losing division of General Motors. In 1987 Roger Penske, a race-car driver, bought a majority stake in the company. As a customer of Detroit Diesel through his truck-leasing business, Penske had definite ideas about what it would take to turn the company around. Essentially, it demanded speeding up production-distribution cycle times and improving customer delivery.

Within months of taking over the company, he invited forty independent distributors to visit Detroit Diesel's new warehouse in Canton, Ohio. He asked them for frank assessments of what they saw, and suggestions on what to change. Out of that visit, the company received 250 suggested changes, which helped cut warehouse delivery time for engine parts from five days to three. Emergency orders were reduced to under twenty-four hours.

To continue the feedback from Detroit Diesel's customers, Penske requires all managers and distributors to call or visit four customers a day to learn about product and service performance.

AMERICAN AIRLINES regularly requests its passengers to evaluate reservations and ticketing, baggage handling, and in-flight services and invites suggestions on how these can be improved. Customer feedback has led to changes in flight scheduling times, seat configuration, extent and variety of in-flight meals and entertainment. It has led to more-geographically-dispersed hubs, updated lounge facilities, and added benefits for frequent fliers.

The point is that customer feedback is essential to determining customer satisfaction. And asking for opinions and suggestions is the quickest way of learning how to improve it.

Customer Feedback Through Customer Complaints

Complaints are grievances or expressions of dissatisfaction by the customer. They arise from:

1. Misunderstandings
2. Erroneous or incomplete information
3. Real or imagined failure by the seller to do or supply what the customer expected

Complaints may arise before or after sale, but regardless of when they arise, they must be addressed. The longer they are ignored or remain unresolved, the more they become a source of lasting friction.

Complaints tend to be viewed negatively. Indeed, in most companies, customer service performance is evaluated by the number of customer complaints received. The higher the number of complaints, the lower the customer service rating. The lower the number of complaints, the higher that rating.

In the sense that complaints reflect customer dissatisfaction, this basis for assessment is understandable. But complaints are also a form of customer feedback. They are a reflection of customer perceptions about supplier performance. As such they are a valuable source of information about shortcomings in that performance and what can be done to improve it.

I know of several companies that actually encourage complaints. Their reasoning is that the more they know about what bothers their customers, the better the understanding the companies get about where and how to satisfy them. Necessarily, this process demands a radical change in philosophy. Instead of keeping score of complaints as a measure of customer service performance, the companies now handle complaints on a "no blame" basis. It's the company as a whole that provides customer service. And pointing fingers of blame when customers are dissatisfied is less constructive than finding out *why* they are dissatisfied and getting on with the task of satisfying them.

1. Customer satisfaction is what the customer says it is. Complaints are expressions of dissatisfaction, so respond to them with all of the interest and concern a dissatisfied customer expects. To do otherwise is to invite loss of the customer.
2. Customer service, as the ensuring of customer satisfaction, is a total company responsibility. It is the achievement not of any one process, function, or activity but of a customer-oriented value network.
3. Customer service as a value-contributing process promotes feedback on customer satisfaction and provides direction to other processes on how to improve satisfaction. Quality and delivery failures are process failures, not people failures; so focus on *what* went wrong and *why*, not on who caused it.

Customer service has been called the customer's ombudsman in the buyer-seller relationship. In its role as the advocate for customer satisfaction, that characterization of customer service is not inappropriate.

Logistics Support

Logistics is the receiving, handling, storing, physical movement, and inventory control of materials and products into, through, and out of the production distribution process. These activities are performed in all companies and in all industries. They may vary in scope and importance by company size and by type of business, but they are common to all. Logistics support therefore is that customer service which speeds up customer logistics, simplifies and improves it, or helps achieve its objectives at lower cost.

Logistics support is the most widely acknowledged value contribution of customer service. In fact, when companies claim to be "added value" sellers, what they usually mean is that over and above their product offerings they also provide logistics support. "Added value" typically refers to customer service features such as:

- Just-in-time delivery programs, which involve making and holding inventory pending customer-scheduled release
- Bonded inventory, which is tested and certified inventory ready for use or further processing
- Consigned or in-plant inventory, which is inventory stocked, dispersed, and replenished by the supplier and paid for only after use
- Conveniently located warehouses and distribution points to facilitate ordering and receipt
- Supplier owned/leased and operated trucks, barges, pipelines, or other modes of transportation to ensure quick and reliable shipment
- Kitting of components to simplify customer handling and routing
- Special packaging and labeling to speed up receipt and storage
- Bar-coding for ease of inspection, handling, and storage
- EDI systems, including terminals at customer sites for order entry and tracking

Obviously, not all markets demand all of these services. And in those markets that do, not all customers perceive them as "added value." What determines the demand for logistics support is:

- The importance of purchased materials as a factor of total product cost, or as a factor of market competitiveness
- The extent and diversity of process steps, from material acquisition to final product sale
- The dynamics of the market, reflecting technological change or supply-demand volatility

The more these factors influence customer buying practice, the greater is the demand for logistics support.

Fortunately, it's precisely in those industries where these factors are critical that customers are most knowledgeable about the impact of logistics services on total customer cost. It is in the electronics, computer, telecommunications, and other high-tech assembly industries that value buying, rather than price buying, is the growing practice. It is in the large-volume retail industry that companies are obsessive about total cost at the point of sale.

Companies that sell in value-conscious markets ignore the importance of logistics support at their own peril. This is particularly true for companies in distribution-type business who sell to OEM or resale customers.

By their very nature, distributors of electronic components, metals, plastics, chemicals, and paper products compete either on price or on the quality of their logistics support. What they sell is, by definition, commodities. Commodities are standardized products sold for general purpose. They are produced and stocked in anticipation of future demand and sold out of existing inventory. As such, they are highly price sensitive. The only way to avoid competing on price is by competing on service. And logistics support services are the prime factor of supplier differentiation.

Metals distribution, for example, is a fiercely competitive industry. Some 650 firms operate 2,000 or so service centers that supply at least a third of the annual U.S. metal demand. The pressure among distributors to differentiate themselves is intense. However, knowing how to differentiate demands getting back to basics about the distribution business.

According to Norman Gottschalk, president of Marmon-Keystone, a large steel and aluminum distributor:

> Distribution is having inventory on the shelf. . . . Too many service center managers forget the business they are in, which is to have metal products available for their customers. People talk about price, service, and delivery as major buying influences, but none of that comes into play unless you have availability.[5]

In the metals distribution industry, differentiation comes from the extent and quality of logistics services over and above assured availability. Such services include metal processing like blanking, cutting to length, sawing, shearing and slitting to reduce customer processing, handling, and routing time. They include identification marking and bar-coding to simplify receiving, inspection, and storing. They include packing, interleaving, and exterior bundle protection to prevent metal damage in shipping and handling.

Reflecting the increasing importance of logistics services in metals distribution, George Von Arx, president of Jorgensen Steel and Aluminum of Brea, California, puts it this way: "We can't just say 'we sell metals' because that's not what we do. We provide a toolbox full of services to the customer. We buy for him, manage his inventory, do some processing for him, handle his [metals] quality control, provide him with on-time deliveries. . . ."[6]

As competition in customer markets grows more intense, demand for logistics support services will accelerate. Distributors in all product fields will have to fashion bigger toolboxes to provide more logistics service if they expect to survive, let alone grow, in the evolving market environment.

Leveraging Logistics

The more closely supplier services are integrated with the customer's engineering, manufacturing, acquistion/logistics, and marketing processes, the greater is their value contribution. This fact is implicit in the growing employment of customer service concepts known as channel integration and supply chain management. Although each concept may have some unique elements, both employ advanced information technology to implement just-in-time and total quality objectives. Both aim for quick response to customer demand through integrated inventory management.

Channel integration is employed in distribution and retail businesses. It relies on customers sharing information at the point of sale with their suppliers, thus enabling suppliers to produce and ship only what is needed. For example, when the retail customer makes a purchase at the store counter, the information is recorded by means of a bar code attached to the purchased item. The clerk at the checkout station scans the code and the point-of-sale information is transmitted electronically to the store's supplier. From these data the supplier knows which products are selling at which stores, which products need replenishment, and which products must be scheduled for manufacture to ensure replenishment as and when needed.

Eastman Kodak sells its photographic equipment and supplies through retail outlets like K-Mart. With K-Mart it has implemented channel integration. Sales information is transmitted electronically to Eastman Kodak headquarters in Rochester, New York. On the basis of that information, Kodak promptly ships to meet store requirements.

In the past, the company shipped to individual stores, often in less than truckload quantities. Through channel integration, Kodak now ships in full truckloads to K-Mart's warehouse and distribution centers. There, in a "cross-dock" operation, shipments are broken down by product and reassembled into outbound loads for individual stores.

K-Mart enjoys the benefits of rapid inventory replenishment, at prices reflecting large-volume shipment. Kodak enjoys the benefit of higher inventory turns, smoother manufacturing cycles, and lower costs of transportation. In a very real sense this integration of K-Mart and Kodak inventory and logistics management enhances both value given and value received. This is an essential ingredient for a true partnership relationship. And channel integration cannot be successfully implemented without that relationship.

Becton-Dickinson is a leading manufacturer of medical supplies and laboratory diagnostic products. It sells direct and through distributors in the health care field worldwide. The company calls its approach to improved customer satisfaction supply chain management (SCM). SCM is "developing a partnership with . . . distributors and customers with the purpose of creating an integrated supply pipeline that will deliver the best products and services at the lowest total system cost."[7]

BD supply chain management employs advanced information technology and integrated logistics to supply a guaranteed level of customer service. Electronically, the system facilitates customer order entry, advanced shipment notification, invoicing, contract and pricing information, rebates and net billing.

Logistically, SCM enables the company to respond as a "single source" supplier of products from multiple product divisions. It permits consolidating and palletizing shipments for ease of handling and storing. It guarantees rapid response to customer demand, reduced cycle times, error-free and damage-free shipments.

Ultimately, the company's goal is the "joint management" of service level improvements and inventory deployment between Becton-Dickinson and the distributors. This encompasses the concept of "automatic replenishment of distributor stock . . . and the establishment of a common data base and shared information systems."[8]

This is a challenging task, made even more challenging by the regulatory and economic problems confronting the health care industry. But as Alfred Battaglia, Becton-Dickinson's group president, puts it:

> Having the best, highest quality products is not enough in today's environment. With great frequency and intensity, our customers are demanding that products be made available to them when and where they need them. Customers expect our products to be delivered in

perfect condition. They expect excellent documentation regarding product use.[9]

I believe that Al Battaglia, as the driving force behind BD supply chain management, is capable of meeting both the challenge and the task.

Customer-Satisfaction Guarantee

Since satisfaction is personal and perceived, companies, in the literal sense, can hardly guarantee it. All they can do is strive for continuous improvement in meeting customer demands more reliably, more cost-effectively.

As a customer service process, however, guarantees are meaningful and relevant. They are promises made to do or supply what the customer specified. They represent commitments made at the time of sale to be fully honored after sale. They are after-sale services that provide substantive meaning to ensuring customer satisfaction with company product and service offerings.

For example:

- When the customer buys a dishwasher, an automobile, or any piece of operating equipment, there is an implied guarantee that it will work. Making it work may demand supplier support in installation, preparation, setup or start-up, and training and monitoring of customer personnel. These are all activities of the satisfaction-guarantee process.

- Office machines, factory equipment, manufacturing systems, and data processing systems experience wear and tear in day-to-day use. To keep them functional and fully operative may require preventive maintenance, spare-parts replacement inventories, and scheduled and emergency repair services. These too are activities of the satisfaction-guarantee process.

- Products become obsolete. Often their inventories prove excessive. In some cases, as with hazardous materials, their disposal demands highly specialized handling or treatment. Replacing products, providing credits or allowances for their trade-in, and removing and disposing of them are still additional activities of the satisfaction-guarantee process.

General Electric has long been a proponent of strong customer guarantees. As a major supplier to electric utilities, it has been particularly attentive to this important customer base. GE's lighting systems department in Hendersonville, North Carolina, supplies its Luminaire lighting products to utilities with the following guarantee, called GE's "Utility Pledge."

GE Lighting Systems pledges to:

- Provide undeniable premium service to you in lighting transactions
- Commit to the highest quality standards in the lighting industry by being the first to offer a five-year warranty on products and components
- Share with you our best practices in forecasting, scheduling, inventory control, packaging and warehousing to help lower your costs and improve your service to customers
- Offer you an 800 number toll-free direct access phone service to our factory for product information, order status and entry, stock status and in-warranty claims and returns
- Invest in inventory dedicated to your account
- Offer on-site training to your distribution crews in Luminaire maintenance and troubleshooting.
- Offer factory expert lighting application of systems and training to achieve optimum lighting design for your customers

At General Electric's motor departments, the company's commitment to customer satisfaction is implemented through a simple yet meaningful practice. Customer service representatives are authorized to approve customer returns for immediate credit regardless of the reason. They don't ask for detailed explanations nor do they need higher-management consent. Distributor customers can return motors two times a year. OEM customers can return them at any time. There are few questions, and there is no hassle.

L. L. Bean, the Freeport, Maine, mail-order house, has achieved a national reputation for its guarantee. It promises "100 percent satisfaction in every way." And it backs its promise with deeds. Customers can return L. L. Bean boots at any time and receive the option of replacement, credit, or refund. Even when living up to its guarantee was painful, the company has done so.

In 1988, dissatisfied customers returned $82 million worth of goods. This represented 14 percent of Bean's total sales and $2 million in return freight charges. Sixty-five percent of the returns were for wrong sizes, and the balance were for quality and other reasons. To correct these problems the company made extensive changes in its production and distribution processes and re-trained its 3,200 employees in quality-improvement methods. However, during all this time, Bean's guarantee commitment remained intact.

Although Bean's experience is not typical, it does dramatize some important points about guarantees and customer satisfaction:

1. Guarantees are no substitute for product and service excellence. What satisfies customers is having their quality, delivery, and service requirements met reliably and consistently. If this is not done, guarantees are meaningless. If this is not done but guarantees are honored—as was the case with Bean—they can be very costly.

2. Guarantees are merely one element of customer service. As such, they should reflect the same strategic considerations we employ in establishing customer information exchange or logistics support systems.

- Does the market or customer acknowledge guarantees as a real value contribution? Do they recognize how guarantees ensure requirement satisfaction? Do they recognize their impact on customer cost, customer revenue, or cash flow?
- Does competition provide the same or comparable guarantees? Will a stronger or more comprehensive guarantee

make for real differentiation between your competition and you?

- What guarantees can you make, given the infrastructure and financial resources you have to support them? To provide what you're not capable of providing or what is too costly to provide means loss of credibility. And loss of credibility can mean loss of customer.
- Which customers provide the best payback potential if you improve guarantees—key accounts, potential partners, those in particular market niches? Will the return be worth the investment?

3. Recognize that when you make guarantees, you're making commitments. Regardless of whether they're legally binding or not, they're representations about what you sell, promises to do what you say. Therefore:

- Make those commitments clear and unambiguous.
- Make them significant and worthy of a customer's consideration.
- Make them easy to implement, with provisions that allow the customer to gain satisfaction easily.
- Above all, make only those commitments you're certain you can honor.

Chapter 8
Putting It All Together

In Chapters 3 through 7 I have addressed the five value-creating and value-adding processes that compose a company's value network: marketing, engineering, acquisition, manufacturing, and customer service. In this final chapter I address what management must do to integrate these processes successfully for value results.

In 1991 John Fluke Manufacturing was a company whose core business was fast eroding. The cause was rapidly changing markets and technology. Founded in 1948, the company manufactured power meters and other measuring devices for the aerospace and other high-tech industries. But with more design work being done by computer modelling techniques, Fluke's test instruments were rapidly becoming obsolete. Further, where its customers were formerly design engineers on R&D projects, they were now service technicians working on cable TV systems, fax machines, and automotive equipment.

To revive this ailing instrument maker, the board of directors appointed Bill Parzybok, a division president at Hewlett-Packard, as Fluke's CEO. Within months, Parzybok put the company through what was called "reverse engineering." This was a critical analysis of Fluke's organizational structure, its processes, its product, market, and customer mix. The aim of this exercise was "reengineering," that is, putting the pieces of the business back together again for improved performance.

Before he changed a thing, however, Parzybok asked managers and employees to define the company's basic values and to project a vision of the company for the future. To some this may sound simplistic, even naïve, but Parzybok has no apologies: "Visions are outwardly focused. If you don't have one, you get to be inwardly focused, and people will fight over how big their piece of the pie is. When you get people focused on customers, it has a very positive, remarkable effect."[1]

I relate this story because it expresses a basic principle about business and the managing of business. To be successful, a company needs a conceptual framework to define what it is and where it's going. Before it can address, in meaningful terms, matters like organizational structure, marketing strategy, resource allocation, or any other area of management concern, a company must establish a reason for being.

That rationale should be realistic and practical, not theoretical. It should be clear and easy to understand, yet compelling enough to implement. It should be flexible, that is, capable of adjusting to the most extreme changes in the business environment. And for a rationale to meet these criteria, necessarily it must be customer focused.

In this book I have proposed what I believe is such a rationale. It is to supply customer value. *Value* I have defined as the satisfaction of customer requirements at least cost of acquisition, ownership, and use. Implicitly, that goes beyond mere low price. It encompasses all customer costs in acquiring, using, maintaining, and replacing what the customer buys. Supplying value means that what we supply:

1. Satisfies customer demands for quality, quantity, time, and service performance, reliably and consistently
2. Satisfies those demands cost-effectively, which means that it:
   - Reduces cost to the customer
   - Avoids cost to the customer
   - Offsets cost by increasing customer revenue or improving customer cash flow

This, I submit, is a powerful and driving "vision"—to borrow Fluke's CEO's term—for managing a business. It is totally customer focused. It does not embrace internally motivating goals like improved efficiency, increased market share, or higher profits. These are results. These are the consequences of being customer focused. They follow from successfully satisfying customer requirements. They follow from being cost-effective.

This vision, this rationale, is also compelling, yet highly flexible. It's compelling because value is acknowledged or perceived by the customer. And it is acknowledged or perceived in a competitive marketplace. So this rationale recognizes the fact that to be successful we must also be competitive. And if we can't compete, we're history.

This rationale is flexible because it is adaptable to all business environments. Regardless of technological change, economic fluctuations, or regulatory demands, the objectives remain the same: to satisfy customer requirements and to do so at least total customer cost.

No Leadership, No Value Results

A company implements this rationale through what I've called a value network. Managing that network is integrating and meshing value-creating and value-adding processes for value results. This demands consideration of organizational structure, information exchange, and measurements of performance against plan. But to implement these and make them meaningful demands leadership: leadership to articulate the value rationale, leadership to guide and direct managers and employees to execute it. And leadership flows from the chief executive down.

It is almost impossible to identify companies that are strongly customer-value focused that do not demonstrate that kind of leadership. We saw it vividly in Ray Kroc, the late founder of McDonald's. His commitment to customer value built a small hamburger outlet into a $7.5 billion international fast-food chain today. That leadership was almost legendary in Sam Walton, the founder of Wal-Mart. His dedication to providing low price with superior service built Wal-Mart into a company creating more jobs since its founding than any other company in America.

We saw that leadership in Bob Galvin, former CEO of Motorola and now chairman of its executive committee. He launched the company on its drive for Six Sigma quality in manufacturing, that is, 3.4 defective parts per million, or near perfection. The company has not achieved Six Sigma as yet, but its level of customer satisfaction is second to none. It's unmatched not only on quality but on delivery and service support as well. And Motorola has more than held its own in meeting price competition.

Leadership does not necessarily mean being liked or being a nice guy. Andy Grove, CEO of Intel, is far from humble and not overly sensitive to people's feelings. But he is a leader and inspires others to follow his lead. Intel is at the cutting edge of computer technology. And Grove has successfully led the company in identifying next-generation customer requirements and satisfying them cost-effectively.

Herb Kelleher, CEO of Southwest Airlines, has been described as a "zany character," and with good reason: "One Easter he walked the plane's aisle clad in an Easter bunny suit. And one St. Patrick's Day, he dressed as a leprechaun."[2] But make no mistake, Kelleher is a leader and he knows where he's leading. Southwest is a low-fare, no-frills airline dedicated to on-time departure and arrival. It has the fewest customer complaints among all airlines, and, uniquely, it has been profitable every year since 1972.

The list goes on of companies that are customer-value oriented and whose senior management leadership has provided the necessary direction and drive:

MICROSOFT, the world's largest independent developer of computer software, and its brilliant founder and CEO, Bill Gates

FEDERAL EXPRESS and its CEO, Fred Smith, who had the foresight and vigor to create the overnight package delivery industry

ADVANCED MICRO DEVICES, by its own characterization, "the second source for semiconductors designed by other companies,"[3] and its flamboyant founder and CEO, Jerry Sanders

The companies and industries are different; certainly the personalities are different. But customer focused companies are led by CEOs with a deep conviction about customer value. They may not express it in the exact words I've used to define that term, but its meaning is clear in actions like these:

- They pay close attention to market and technological developments, and carefully assess the effect of those developments on customer requirements.
- They set priorities and allocate resources with the aim of meeting those requirements to full customer satisfaction.
- They are acutely conscious of customer cost. If price is the dominant customer-cost concern, they surpass in price competitiveness. If it is not, they strive for least total costs through product performance and quality, assurance of supply, technical services, and market support.

In all cases, these CEOs have a clear vision for the company they lead and the charisma and drive to make that vision a reality. Everything begins with that.

Building the Value Network

A company implements the value rationale through its value network. This is the structure that meshes value-creating and value-adding processes for value results.

The first step in building that structure is redefining the meaning of *work* and redesigning how it's performed. From the days of Fredrick Taylor until only recently, the accepted wisdom was to break work down into specialized functions and then organize the business around them. Authority and decision-making flowed from the chief executive, through functional management, down to "workers" performing functional jobs and tasks.

We have already seen how this business and management model is out of date. It is incapable of dealing with today's realities of rapidly changing technology, steadily shortening product life cycles, heightened competition—globally and by market segment—and increasing sophistication and assertiveness of customers and markets. It is incapable of dealing with these realities because our notion of work—productive work in the business sense—is faulty.

Products are not designed to meet today's performance and time demands in an engineering vacuum. Nor are they sourced, manufactured, marketed, or supported by other functions similarly independent and removed from a larger scene. The work that produces business results is performed not through functions but through processes. This is not an idle play on words. Functions are specialized activities. Processes are systems, that is, combinations of functions. Processes are complex and continuously evolving. They cut across functional lines, so that they demand horizontal as well as vertical integration.

This fact is recognized in a management concept gaining increasing attention. It's called reengineering or process redesign. The term *reengineering* was introduced by Michael Hammer, a management consultant, in 1990. And his ideas have been well publicized since then.

Reengineering is, in theory, revamping a business, starting it over from scratch. By critically reviewing everything a company does, reengineering aims to recombine distinct yet related activities into fewer but more-efficient processes. As a successful application of reengineering, Mr. Hammer cites Ford's redesign of its accounts payable procedures. Where it once employed 500 people to handle purchase orders and invoices, it now employs 125 people, who do the same job faster.

Reconstructing a business into a value network is indeed reengineering. It's reassessing and reorganizing activities and functions in terms of their value contribution. It's recombining them into value-creating and value-adding processes. It's meshing these processes into an integral business system. Thus, it is reengineering, but reengineering with a difference. It is reengineering that is tightly focused, customer-value focused.

Reengineering processes into a value network does not aim for efficiency or improved productivity to satisfy internal concerns. If these are valid objectives, it's because they are necessary means to satisfying customer requirements cost-effectively. The entire thrust of the value network is to redirect effort and resources from internal to external goals. What does the customer demand? What does competition supply? What combination of product and service can we supply that will satisfy customer demands at least total cost of acquisition, ownership, and use?

As I've stated earlier, it takes strong and dedicated senior management, first to acknowledge the customer-value rationale, and then to keep the company on track to implement it.

Structuring the Value Network

The first time I visited with Amgen, the very successful biotechnology company, I asked to see an organizational chart. I was told that Amgen doesn't publish an organizational chart. Undoubtedly it has one, but it just doesn't circulate it.

The company is highly informal, with an aversion to rigid structure and hierarchy. Of course it has departments and position titles, but these do not define how work gets done. The company is program and project oriented, and it employs cross-functional and cross-discipline teams to achieve results. It is not uncommon for scientists, engineers, and business specialists to participate on several teams at the same time. Nor is it uncommon for team members to change roles from one program or project to another.

For a company to operate as a value network, it must employ a fluid organizational structure, not unlike that of the Amgen pattern. The structure must be flexible and adaptable, not constrained by functional charter or confining job descriptions. It must be elastic, allowing for the network to expand or contract as market or technology demands require. It must be collegial, not hierarchical, with no process having primacy in the network structure, with processes attaining primacy only as customer requirements dictate. It is only by organizing along these lines that a company can promote the interaction and interconnectivity that are the essential features of a true value network.

In Chapter 2, I referred to customer-focused teams as microcosms of the value network. They're microcosms because they epitomize the network both in purpose and in structure.

When teams are formed to reduce customer cost or speed up customer delivery times, they're pursuing, on a smaller scale, the same objectives of the value network. Teams combine multifunction members who interact and interrelate outside the formal departmental framework. On a much larger scale, the value network acts the same way. Instead of integrating functions, it integrates processes. It integrates and meshes them into a customer-value-focused system, which operates outside or in tandem with the formal company organization.

A microcosm is not a universe, and teams—even customer-oriented teams—do not constitute a value network. But without question, they provide the building blocks for structuring one. By continuously identifying customer cost and performance needs, and creating teams to satisfy them, a company transforms itself into a value network.

The process is not immediate; it's gradual. And it doesn't work unless team goals are specific and measurable. Their achievement must also make a difference—a difference in how the customer perceives us, a difference in our ability to compete effectively. Goals that do that are ones like reducing delivery time from seven days to forty-eight hours; achieving a zero defect rate on all customer shipments; reducing customer costs in receiving and handling by 50 percent. Setting goals that are fuzzy or incapable of measurement does not further the value network's structure; it merely trivializes the team approach.

But for teams to be effective there must be teamwork at the senior management level. If people at the top cannot interrelate, if they cannot subordinate narrow functional interests for a common customer-value goal, it's not likely that teams at the operating level can be successful. And this is more of a problem than managements are willing to admit. Peter M. Senge of MIT's Sloan School of Management refers to "the myth of the management team." According to Senge, "All too often [management] teams in business spend their time fighting for turf, avoiding anything that will make them look bad personally, and pretending that everyone is behind the team's collective strategy—maintaining the appearance of a cohesive team."[4]

If for no other reason, the massive drive toward staff reductions and downsizing has had a positive effect. It has removed layers of management and supervision between those who plan and those who implement. It has eliminated fiefdoms and bureaucracies whose sole reason for being is to be self-perpetuating. It has eliminated activities that contribute little or no customer value, and promoted their outsourcing on an "as and when needed" basis. It has reduced companies to more-manageable proportions and in so doing brought them closer to the market and the customer.

Information Technology Makes It All Possible

Not too long ago, it would have been pure fantasy to theorize about the value network, let alone propose it as a practical business and management model. Not so today! The advancements we've made in information technology make that model attainable. From personal computers to cellular phones, from faxes and modems to hand-held scanners, we can move information over and through the total business spectrum, and do it in real time.

Information that took researchers and analysts weeks to assemble is now at our fingertips with a click of a switch. Data that took clerks and typists days to compile, record and transmit are now on computer databases and readily accessible in seconds. Advancements in hardware are matched by advancements in software. Indeed, it is the synergy between hardware and software that propels information technology. It is no exaggeration to say that what this allows is a total change in how we think about business and the management of business. It allows us, for the first time, to be truly customer focused:

■ Where only seven years ago, Hewlett-Packard sales representatives spent a mere 26 percent of their time with customers, they now spend nearly 40 percent. The reason is that they're equipped with portable computers and electronic messaging devices. This now links them to the company's field sales, product marketing, order processing, even corporate marketing units. If one department cannot handle a customer inquiry, the inquiry is switched in seconds to a department or office that can. This is important if a company is to be customer focused.

■ Air Products and Chemicals of Allentown, Pennsylvania, had a chronic inability to keep up with customer telephone orders. Its forty inside sales reps were spending less time talking to customers than they were spending checking customer accounts and faxing messages to the company's plants and warehouses to determine product availability. Instead of incurring the expense of developing a specially designed data system, Air Products bought a UNIX database from a competitor and modified it.

When sales reps now receive a customer inquiry they go to a PC-based interactive program. It's staffed by two engineers who, through an applications-specific dialogue, answer 70 percent of all customer questions. Ten percent of those questions require contact with the company's labs or plants, and all answers they provide are stored in the database for future use. This both simplifies and speeds up the process of defining and specifying customer needs.

■ When computer-aided design (CAD) first came on the scene, it required the power of large mainframe computers to implement. This tended to limit its application to large companies that could afford them. Also, early CAD systems—particularly those small companies could afford—merely produced a set of drawings. Production engineers had to develop the geometry of volume and density, and this was often done manually.

Today, CAD is workstation or PC based. It's integrated with computer-aided manufacturing (CAM), so that product design and production design are performed concurrently. This reduces cycle time of design, through manufacturing, to customer delivery. It also improves customer quality because designs for product are also designs for producibility.

■ Customer manufacturing has always posed problems for

companies that sell both a standard line of product and customer-specified applications of the product. They must plan and schedule both by customer order and by common materials and facility resources to satisfy each market segment. MRP systems are materials driven and work well for the standard product. Alone, they don't work as well on customized orders. However, MRP systems can be complemented by job-order software to control custom jobs on a job-routing basis. Systems that do this employ the MRP bill of materials for standard parts, then plan, schedule, and expedite related subassemblies and assemblies as specific requirements of each job.

With existing technology, in the form of commercially available software, workstations, PCs, and terminals, this is readily achievable. The payoff is close integration of procurement and manufacturing to control both production for inventory and production for custom orders. The real payoff is improved customer satisfaction in both market segments.

Information is the lifeblood of the value network, and it comes from external as well as internal sources. Customers provide information and feedback on product quality and delivery performance. This is vital to future design and production effort. Suppliers provide technology transfer, quality and delivery intelligence, performance and progress reports. It is only through timely and error-free exchange of data and documentation that these external sources can be meshed with internal ones for improved value results.

Companies in consumer and distribution markets have known this for years. Through electronic data interchange (EDI) systems and sophisticated bar-code technology, they have integrated customers and suppliers into their tightly meshed value network. Wal-Mart, K-Mart, Target Stores, Arrow Electronics, and Avnet have been highly successful in making this happen. Service companies like American Express, Federal Express, and American Airlines have employed information technology successfully in integrating their customer base, but less successfully with their supply base. It is in the manufacturing sector where there has been less success in integrating customers and suppliers with internal value-contributing sources. With the exception of a few score companies, notably ones like Hewlett-Packard, AT&T, General Electric, Xerox, Motorola, Ford Motor, much remains to be to be done to employ information exchange to integrate customers and suppliers within the value network.

The information technology is there to do it, even if it's as elemental as using PCs, faxes, and bar codes to facilitate the data flow. What's lacking is the vision of where the effort could lead, and the leadership to drive toward that goal rather than dwell on day-to-day operational problems.

It's the Accounting, Stupid!

Supplying customer value is not a difficult concept to accept in theory. The difficulty lies in implementing it. It lies in identifying and quantifying customer perceptions of value, structuring processes that create and add value into a value-supply network, and managing that network for value results. Achieving any of these objectives demands meaningful information exchange between customers and company, company and suppliers, between and among internal activities, functions, and processes. As I've already pointed out, the technology for effecting the mechanics of that exchange already exists. The problem lies in the design and content of the information itself. Much of it is not meaningful. And where this problem is most pronounced is in the area of cost information: cost as a company accounts for it, cost as the customer might acknowledge or perceive it.

Traditional cost-accounting methods have been around for the past seventy-five to eighty years. They evolved as industry evolved, from simple craft-type manufacturing to mass production. They were developed to support manufacturing of standardized products in an environment of stable or slow-to-change technology. They were based on the assumption that production was labor intensive, and that price was the only cost customers acknowledged. Thus, the accounting system was designed to promote labor efficiency, which in turn would promote price competitiveness.

Under traditional systems, direct labor is the base for allocating manufacturing overhead. Costing out products means assigning supervision, inspection, machine setup, materials handling and storing, and other expenses on the basis of their direct labor content. The measurements that the system provides for management control are direct labor hours, machine utilization, and period-end overhead absorption.

With a cost system so structured, there is every incentive for management to keep machines and manpower busy, even if that means creating excess or obsolete inventory. There is every incentive to turn out more and more product, even if it is faulty or out of spec. The higher the rate of production, the more "efficient" labor appears. The higher the rate of production, the more "favorably" we absorb manufacturing overhead.

Current systems account for costs only as they are identified. They cannot deal with costs that are not identified, such as the costs of failure. The cost of:

- Not producing in the quantity and at the time specified
- Not meeting customer design, performance, or reliability requirements
- Not providing after-sale product or technical support

Current systems poorly account for research and development, marketing and sales expense, and customer service. They lump these costs into overhead pools, which are allocated against total cost of product or production. The formula for allocation is arbitrary, reflecting neither how a product incurs these costs nor how customer requirements demand them.

It is truly amazing that we employ these dated accounting practices in view of the radical changes we've seen in the business and technical environment. Over the past fifty years direct labor and manufacturing has declined from 75 percent of product cost to 12 percent. For companies in advanced technology industry, it can be as low as 5 to 8 percent. Companies are less vertically integrated, buying more materials and components from outside suppliers and increasingly outsourcing manufacturing and engineering. Technology has exploded, creating new products in ever shortening time cycles. Markets have become segmented and specialized and are competitive on both a local and global basis. Customers are cost conscious, not only in terms of price but in terms of total costs in use.

To adapt to these changes, we have reorganized into leaner and more-flexible operating units. We have promoted concurrent or simultaneous engineering to incorporate advanced technology faster in new-product design and manufacturing. To implement that concept we have created cross-functional design and worker teams. We have introduced MRP, total quality management, and just-in-time techniques to become more responsive to market and customer demands. And to achieve all this we've employed the full array of information hardware and software technology. Yet despite these changes, many of them drastic and certainly not all of them universally adopted, one thing remains the same: how we identify and account for cost.

Why Do We Account for Cost?

Companies employ cost information for two basic purposes. The first is to report operating results of profit and loss to shareholders, creditors, and tax collecting agencies. The second is to provide management with the data to determine product cost and to plan for future investment. Twenty years ago, even ten years ago, traditional accounting methods could serve both purposes adequately. Today they cannot. They are misleading in serving the first purpose. They are misleading and potentially catastrophic in serving the second. In terms of a company's ability to function as a value supplier, it is the second purpose that demands our most immediate attention.

Whether by design or intuition, management has long recognized the deficiencies in conventional cost-accounting methods. It has supported the development of management information systems that collect and organize data differently than cost systems do. The aim is to fill information voids and improve the caliber of management judgment. It has encouraged the use of mathematical modelling techniques, which employ cost estimates, income-cost targets, profit and loss projections. The aim is to relate cost to identifiable opportunities, thereby simplifying and speeding up decision-making. Management has even by-passed the cost system when critical strategic considerations demand action and not protracted analysis.

Allen-Bradley is a subsidiary of Rockwell, International, a conglomerate in the aerospace, automotive, and electrical equipment industries. Allen-Bradley competes globally in a volatile, industrial automation market. Its strategy has been to sustain and strengthen its worldwide marketing momentum through state-of-the-art manufacturing. It implemented that strategy through a fifty-machine flexible-assembly complex, not in Manchester or Malaysia, but in Milwaukee, the company's home base. The facility reads parts-assembly requirements from bar codes and produces motor starters in 125 different configurations at the rate of 600 an hour. It has enabled the company to increase export sales fivefold over a six-year period.

Yet, as Tracey O'Rourke, Allen-Bradley's CEO, puts the matter:

> The project might have been at risk if we had approached it in the traditional way. . . . After we decided to make the product here in Milwaukee and compete anywhere on price, the issue was to find the enabling manufacturing strategy. In essence, we "bought" the investment in terms of quality, cost, market share and size, competition and profitability. If there is a time to ignore conventional return-on-assets calculations, it's when your long-term goals are at stake. Justification has to become more of a policy decision than an accounting practice.[5]

Becoming a viable value supplier is a long-term objective. And clearly managing a value network to achieve that goal is anything but an accounting practice. Of course, both demand the consideration of cost—cost as a function of value contribution, cost as a measure of customer satisfaction. These are ways of looking at cost totally different from how we look at it now.

Neither the company nor the product can be the sole "cost center," that is, the base of cost identification and collection. A critical cost base must be the value network, comprising those processes that create and add value as the customer perceives it. And customer cost cannot be price alone; it's price plus all costs incurred in acquiring, using, holding and replacing what the customer buys.

The Concept of Value Costing

Creating a value network calls for organizing activities and functions outside the formal company structure, or in parallel with it. So too does creating a value costing system. It means using information that the accounting system now provides and reorganizing it to be value focused and value specific. For example, customer requirements vary by customer type, channel of distribution, geographical location, order quantities, and extent and levels of customer service. The costs involved in satisfying these requirements are not the same for all customers. Management knows this instinctively, but typical cost systems ignore the fact. By allocating costs that are functions of these requirements arbitrarily against product and volume, they assume that costs are equal regardless of requirement differences.

Value costing captures cost by customer. This does not replace existing methods of costing; it merely adds another dimension of cost identification and allocation to the costing process. Where order entry, warehousing, and shipping costs are measured by labor hours and charged to departments and then to products, under value costing they are treated an additional way. They are compiled and allocated by customer as actually incurred by customer account. They are measured by relevant factors such as purchase orders received, customer orders filled, presale and after-sale customer service support. Again, it is the advancements we've made in information technology that make this feasible. What makes it practicable is providing the customer-value focus to redirect current accounting practice.

ABC and Value Costing

Fortunately, there is an accounting concept that allows us to do what I've just described. It's known as activity-based costing (ABC). ABC was introduced nearly a decade ago by academicians like Dr. Robert Kaplan, then at Sloan Mellon University, Dr. Robin Cooper of the Harvard Business School, and Dr. Tom Johnson of Portland State University. Simultaneously and independently, it was also developed at the John Deere Component Works in Waterloo, Iowa. Activity-based costing is employed at companies like Hewlett-Packard, General Electric, Northern Telecom, Honeywell, and Avery International. Management interest in ABC, as shown by seminars, workshops, and published material, is growing by leaps and bounds.

ABC was developed initially to address the "below-the-line" costs of research and development, marketing and sales, physical distribution and general administration. It was developed to give management a better understanding of how these costs were incurred by product, by market, by channels of distribution.

Today, ABC does a great deal more. It not only tells management what triggers cost, but provides a sounder basis for managing it. By assigning costs to product and customers, based on the resources they consume, ABC improves resource allocation. By identifying activity costs like machine setup, planning and procurement, order scheduling and processing by customer as well as product, ABC allows management to allocate resources for improved value results. For example:

- What activities are involved in shipping product to the customer on a daily rather than a weekly or biweekly basis?
- What is the cost of manpower facilities, trucking, and fuel resources necessary to provide each level of customer service?
- How does each level affect customer costs of receiving, handling, storing, and using?
- What level of service is cost-effective, as the customer acknowledges cost-effectiveness?

By using activity-based costing to determine the costs of both supplying and acquiring, we mesh company and customer within a common value network. Figure 8-1 shows that both customer and company employ value-creating, value-adding processes. These processes consist of activities that consume resources: manpower, material, and capital. The consumption of resources results in cost. In producing to meet customer requirements, the company incurs costs that are a direct function of those requirements. In acquiring what the company supplies, the customer incurs costs that are a function of the supply process.

Figure 8-1. Cost and the value network.

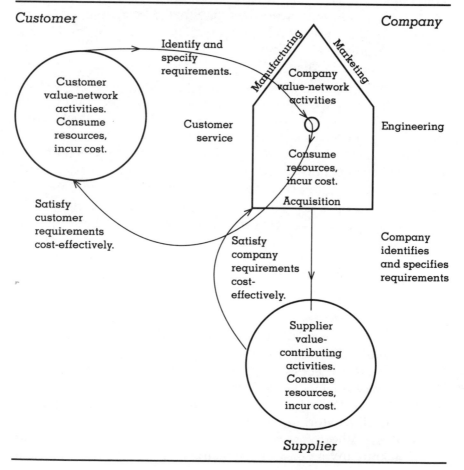

Activity-based costing provides common metrics for quantifying both buyer and seller costs. It also provides common metrics for measuring value given and value received. To the customer that means satisfaction of requirements at least cost of acquisition, ownership, and use. To the company it means satisfactory value in exchange: a competitive price, factored upward to reflect customer cost savings, avoidances, or offsets from increased revenue or improved cash flow; a competitive price in exchange for increased sales volume or increased market share.

At the present time very few companies use activity-based costing as the only accounting system. One notable exception is Hewlett-Packard which uses it as its on-line cost system at many of its division locations. H-P uses ABC for all accounting purposes, including the sensitive one of inventory evaluation. However, the vast majority of companies that use ABC do so primarily for product costing, pricing, make-or-buy decisions, and investment analysis. Their systems are microcomputer based and are employed in conjunction with the more traditional, official cost system.

Ideally, ABC should be the sole accounting system. It can be confusing to have both a conventional and ABC system operating side by side. Further, whether we like it or not, people make decisions on the basis of how they're evaluated. If they're evaluated by criteria the conventional system establishes, they will be wary about making decisions based on ABC analysis. In his book *A Complete Guide to Activity Based Accounting*, Michael O'Guin relates how the engineering department at Tektronix, the Beaverton, Oregon, manufacturer of electronic instrumentation, "refused to use ABC for design decision-making, unless the controller made the system the Company's cost system."[6]

Despite the problems ABC might create, its advantages greatly outweigh its disadvantages. And for achieving what I'm proposing, those advantages are enormous. ABC provides a powerful tool for managing a business as a true value network. By structuring cost information to be customer focused, management can effectively manage for value results. Further, it can often do so without drastic changes.

If a company has a manufacturing resource planning system

(MRP II) in place, it has much of the information activity based costing requires. It has bills of materials and job routings, with tie-ins to the general ledger. Through detailed analysis of how activities and processes work, a company can literally develop a bill of activity (BOA), the labor and machine equivalent of the bill of materials (BOM). Through simulation, it can relate cost data to variables like quantity and volume, changes in product mix, and all the "what-ifs" that can surface in a changing technology and market environment.

That the traditional accounting system is the formal system for measuring profit and loss, asset evaluation, company liabilities, and equity, should not deter the implementation of activity-based costing. Managing for value results is not an accounting exercise. It ought not be constrained by accounting practices whose prime justification is that they're traditional and official.

Alliances and Partnerships and the Value Network

Managing for value results requires integration of customers and suppliers within the value network. This poses problems different from those in integrating internal processes. Customers and suppliers are independent entities. They are buyers of what we sell, sellers of what we buy. They have their own objectives and interests, their own priorities and concerns. These are not identical with ours; indeed, they may conflict. So seeking out customers and selecting suppliers to mesh within the value network must be a careful and deliberate effort.

Within recent years, we've heard much about strategic alliances and buyer-seller partnerships. In a very real sense these are exactly the relationships a company must establish to integrate customers and suppliers within the value network. Therefore, with that objective in mind let me suggest the following conditions such relationships must meet if they are to be successful:

1. There must be a clear definition of purpose and intent in the relationship. With customers, it is to enhance customer value.

With suppliers, it is to complement company technology and resources in satisfying customer requirements cost-effectively. For value given to customers and value received from suppliers, the relationship must provide fair and reasonable value in exchange.

2. The relationship must be ongoing, rather than a one-time or intermittent one. It is created with the intention of surviving over difficult as well as favorable times. It's a relationship established because the parties see mutual benefit resulting from their association.

3. The relationship demands that both parties commit the necessary resources—physical, technical, financial—to the task of achieving their previously defined common objectives.

4. The integration of management and information systems is implicit in this mutual commitment of resources. In a true alliance or partnership, customers don't unilaterally define requirements; nor do suppliers unilaterally decide how and when to satisfy them. These are determined cooperatively and in concert.

5. The mutual commitment of resources demands that both parties provide to each other complete information on relevant plans, progress, and problems. This responsibility lasts from the time the relationship starts until the time it ends. Misinformation, incomplete information, exaggerated claims and promises that cannot be kept are all breaches of faith in alliance and partnering relationships.

6. Customer-company alliances and company-supplier partnerships entail risks. The risks are economic, financial, and technical. They are risks of lost markets and lost opportunities. If these relationships are to be viable, risks must be identified and quantified up front, and provisions must be made to deal with them as and when they occur.

7. Essential to the sharing of risks associated with prices and costs is the demand that customer-supplier partners "open their books" to one another. Customers must identify costs that are affected by supplier quality, time, and service performance. Suppliers must relate the costs of development, production, and

service support to the prices they ask. Pricing within the value network is not competitive pricing; it's pricing that relates cost to value contribution.

8. Customer-supplier relationships are established for mutual benefit. This means there must be an equitable sharing of the value results that flow from that relationship. For the customer-buyer, the sharing is realized through improved product quality, better assurance of supply and the cost savings and avoidances that follow. For the supplier-seller, the sharing may be through increased business volume, longer-term supply agreements, prices based on value contribution, not solely competition.

9. In the course of working within the value network, customers and suppliers employ technology original to each. They also develop technology new to each. At the same time both are exposed to technology change. Successful alliances or partnerships carefully define the substance and terms of technology exchange. That exchange may be one of the prime reasons for the relationship; so it should not be treated lightly.

10. Finally, true partners do not compete with one another. Nor does one enter into multiple partnerships to pursue the same objective. This means that we ought not seek out customers or suppliers to integrate in the value network whose markets, technologies, and strategic interests conflict with ours.

Strategic alliances and partnerships are like marriages: we enter into them for better or for worse. Like marriages that turn out badly, they can be terminated. But we don't enter into marriages or these relationships to terminate them. We do so because we believe they can work, and we intend to make them work.

To Summarize

Managing the value network is planning, organizing, integrating, and measuring those processes that create and add value as the customer acknowledges or perceives it. It is managing human, capital, information, and time resources for value results. This is an externally focused view of management. It aims at customer satisfaction and customer cost containment. This is at odds with traditional views of management that pursue more-narrow company or functional objectives and internal cost control.

To manage a business successfully as a value network demands a reorientation of management perspective from internal to external concerns. It demands a reassessment of functions and activities in terms of customer-value contribution. It demands a restructuring of organization, processes, the very meaning of "work" to be consistent with the value-creating paradigm. In this last chapter I have developed these concepts as imperatives for managing a business as an effective value network.

The Seven Management Imperatives

1. Management must provide a clear vision of the company and a clear rationale for it to follow. The vision is that of a company dedicated to the satisfaction of customer requirements at the least cost of ownership and use. The rationale is that customer value is supplied through a network of internal and external value contributors, closely integrated for value results.

2. Management must provide the leadership to articulate the value concept—internally to managers and employees, externally to customers and suppliers. It must demonstrate that leadership through the commitment and drive to implement the value strategy, despite changes in the technical or business environment.

3. Management must redefine the meaning of work and redesign how it is performed. Work is activities involved in value-creating, value-adding processes. Redesigning work is reengineering activities and processes for value results.

4. Management must structure the value network to be flexible and adaptable, not confined by rigid practice or protocol. Cross-functional teams are microcosms of the value network and provide the organizational model for the network structure.

5. Management must employ information technology to facilitate information exchange and data flow—internally among activities, functions, and processes, externally with customers

and suppliers. Meaningful information exchange is the lifeblood of an effective value network.

6. Management must introduce and implement value costing. Value costing relates activity to value contribution; consumption of resources, or cost, to value results. Value costing makes that relationship internally with value-contributing processes, externally with customers and suppliers. Activity-based costing is the cost discipline for value costing.

7. Management must establish alliances and partnerships to mesh customers and suppliers within the value network. To do this successfully, management must be discriminating in the customers it seeks and the suppliers it selects. It must be attentive to the agenda and details of the agreements it makes to establish the relationships. And management must promote close interaction and cooperation, from the highest level down, between company and customer, company and supplier.

Implementing these imperatives is not an easy task. Certainly it's not a task to be accomplished overnight. But at the same time, it's not as complex—or disruptive—as the facile prescription of starting fresh "with a clean sheet of paper." After all, supplying customer satisfaction is a concept already acknowledged. And although it's acknowledged more often in the abstract than in actual practice, it does provide a common rationale and a common base from which to restructure and build a value-oriented enterprise. The real challenge to management in implementing these imperatives is to flesh out the abstraction of "customer satisfaction" with its essential substance, that is:

- Satisfy customer product, service, technology, and information requirements fully and reliably
- Satisfy them with cost effectiveness in their acquisition, ownership, and use by reducing cost to the customer; by avoiding cost to the customer; and by offsetting customer cost by increasing revenue or improving customer cash flow

Anton Chekhov, the great Russian playwright and novelist, once wrote: "If you cry 'Forward!' you must make plain in what direction you want to go. Don't you see that if without doing so, you call out the word to both monk and revolutionary, they will go in directions precisely opposite."

With those seven imperatives in mind, I say: "Forward to fundamentals!"

Notes

Chapter 1: The Meaning of Value: Managing for Value Results

1. As reported in "Shifting Gears," *Wall Street Journal*, May 7, 1993.
2. As reported in "The Technology Payoff," *Business Week*, June 14, 1993.
3. "Something Rotten in the State of Software," *The Economist*, January 12, 1982.
4. Peter F. Drucker, *Managing for Results* (New York: Harper & Row, 1964), p. 5.
5. Michael E. Porter, *Competitive Advantage* (New York: Free Press, 1985), p. 33.
6. Ibid., p. 38.

Chapter 2: Management and The Value Network

1. *Webster's New College Dictionary*, 3rd ed. (Englewood Cliffs, N.J.: Prentice Hall, 1989).
2. Peter F. Drucker, "Be Data Literate, Know What to Know," *Wall Street Journal*, December 1, 1992.
3. James P. Womack, Daniel T. Jones, and Daniel Roos, *The Machine That Changed the World* (New York: Harpers, 1991), pp. 129–30.
4. Ibid., p. 112–13.

Chapter 3: Marketing and Value

1. "More and More Retail Giants Rule the Marketplace," *Business Week*, December 21, 1992.

2. As quoted in "What Price Glory?" *The Economist*, 1991.
3. Theodore Levitt, "Marketing Myopia," *Harvard Business Review*, September/October 1975.
4. "Staying Power," *Wall Street Journal*, December 9, 1992.
5. J. D. Staunton, "Total Planning for Selling Value," National Society of Sales Training Executives, September 1988.
6. Texas Instruments advertisement, *Wall Street Journal*, Nov. 3, 1987.
7. Source: CMP Publications Incorporated (New York: Technology Research Center, 1992).
8. Distributor Survey, *Electronic Buyers News*, June 1992.
9. Arrow/Schweber mailer, "Focused on Satisfaction," New York, 1991.
10. Distributor Survey, *Electronic Buyers News*, December 7, 1992.

Chapter 4: Value and the Engineering Process

1. R. L. Leibensperger, "Power Density-Product Design for the Twenty-First Century," Timken Corporation, Canton, Ohio, 1991.
2. Ibid.
3. As reported in *Computer Reseller News*, January 18, 1993.
4. "IBM Bends Its Rules to Make a Laptop," *Wall Street Journal*, April 19, 1991.
5. As quoted in *Electronics Purchasing*, November 1992.
6. Ibid.
7. As reported in *Electronic Buyers News*, July 6, 1992.
8. Computer-Aided Manufacturing, International, Inc., as reported in "A Smarter Way to Manufacture," *Business Week*, April 30, 1990.
9. Dataquest, as reported in "A Smarter Way to Manufacture," *Business Week*, April 30, 1990.
10. National Institute of Standards and Technology, Thomas Group, Inc., Institute of Defense Analysis, as reported in "A Smarter Way to Manufacture," *Business Week*, April 30, 1990.
11. "Engineering: Where Competitive Success Begins," *Industry Week*, November 1990.

Chapter 5: Value and the Acquisition Process

1. "Top 100," *Purchasing*, November 22, 1990.
2. As reported in *The Economist*, March 3, 1991.
3. As reported in "How Baldrige Buyers Slay Cost," *Electronics Purchasing*, January 1993.
4. Ibid.

5. As quoted in "The Extended Enterprise," *Purchasing*, March 4, 1993.
6. As quoted in "Doing What You Do Best," *Traffic Management*, July 1992.

Chapter 6: Manufacturing as a Value-Creating Process

1. "When GM's Robots Ran Amok," *The Economist*, 1991.
2. "Reinventing America," *Business Week*, 1992.
3. As reported in "Duel," *The Economist*, 1992.
4. As reported in "IBM—An Honest Attempt to Crown the Customer King," *Computer Reseller News*, January 20, 1993.
5. "Duel."
6. "IBM—An Honest Attempt. . . ."
7. "Future Factories," *Wall Street Journal*, January 13, 1993.
8. Ibid.

Chapter 7: Value and the Customer Service Process

1. *A Guide to Customer Satisfaction* (Stamford, Conn.: Learning International, 1990).
2. S. J. Diamond, "Consumer Affairs," *L.A. Times*, August 15, 1991.
3. *Focus on Satisfaction* (New York: Arrow Electronics, 1992).
4. As reported in "King Customer," *Business Week*, March 12, 1990.
5. "Distributors Scramble to Satisfy Buyer Demands," *Purchasing*, May 6, 1993.
6. Ibid.
7. *Supply Chain Management*, Becton-Dickinson (Franklin Lakes, N.J.: 1990).
8. Ibid.
9. Ibid.

Chapter 8: Putting It All Together

1. As reported in "John Fluke Manufacturing," *Fortune*, March 22, 1993.
2. R. Levering and M. Moskowitz, *The 100 Best Companies in America* (New York: Currency-Doubleday, 1992), p. 413.
3. Ibid., p. 5.
4. As reported in "Team Work Starts at the Top," *Fortune*, April 1991.
5. As reported in "Automation and the Bottomline," *Industry Week*, May 26, 1986.
6. Michael O'Guin, *A Complete Guide to Activity Based Accounting* (Englewood Cliffs, N.J.: Prentice Hall, 1991), p. 57.

Index